the
JOB BOOK
100 Acting Jobs
For Actors

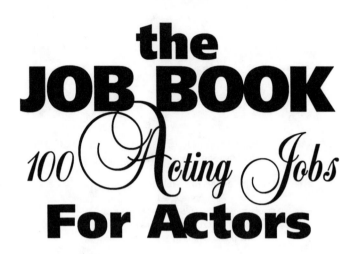

the JOB BOOK
100 Acting Jobs For Actors

Edited by Glenn Alterman

A Career Development Book

SK

A Smith and Kraus Book

Published by Smith and Kraus, Inc.
One Main Street, Lyme, NH 03768

Copyright © 1995 by Smith and Kraus, Inc.
All rights reserved
Manufactured in the United States of America
Cover and Text Design by Julia Hill
Cover photo ©1995 by Sue Bennett

First Edition: May 1995
10 9 8 7 6 5 4 3 2 1

Library of Congress Cataloging-in-Publication
Alterman, glenn, 1946-
    The job book: 100 acting jobs for actors / by Glenn Alterman.
        p. cm. -- (A career development book)
        ISBN 1-880399-81-4 (alk. paper)

    1. Acting--Vocational guidance. 2. Performing arts--Vocational guidance. I. Title. II. Title: 100 acting jobs for actors. IV. Series.

PN2055.A45   1994
792'.028'023--dc20   94-46978
                  CIP

This book is for my friends
Eva Charney and Joe Sullivan

Contents

BIOGRAPHY

Glenn Alterman is the author of *Street Talk, Uptown*, and the recently released, *Two Minutes and Under*. *Street Talk* and *Uptown* were both featured selections of the Doubleday's Fireside Theater Book Club. *Two Minutes and Under* recently went into its second printing. His play *Nobody's Flood* has won the Bloomington Playwrights Project Playwriting Competition and was a finalist in the Key West Theater Festival. Alterman's play *Like Family* has been optioned by Red Eye Productions to be made into a movie. *The Danger of Strangers* is presently a finalist in the George R. Kernodle Playwriting Competition. *Heartstrings—The National Tour*, commissioned by the Design Industries Foundation for AIDS (DIFFA), received a 30 city tour with a cast of 35 including Michelle Pfeiffer, Ron Silver, Christopher Reeve, Susan Sarandon, Marlo Thomas and Sandy Duncan. His play *Goin' Round on Rock Solid Ground* was a finalist at The Actors Theater of Louisville and subsequently received productions at the Circle Rep Lab and The West Bank Cafe Downstairs Theater Bar. His plays *Toxic Redemption* and *Coulda-Woulda-Shoulda* were performed at festivals at Primary Stages in New York. His other plays have been performed at La Mama, The Nat Horne Theater, Playwrights Horizons and Circle Rep Lab in New York, as well as at the Beverly Hills Rep (Theater Forty) and West Coast Ensemble theaters in Los Angeles. Mr. Alterman is presently working on several other books for Smith and Kraus including the soon to be released *What to Get Your Agent For Christmas (and 100 Other Suggestions for Actors)*.

ACKNOWLEDGEMENTS

The author wishes to thank the following:
Joanne Curley, Wendy Cole (*Grace Under Fire*), David Roos (The Gilla Roos Agency), Leslie (Hoban) Blake, Les McDonough, Gloria Slofkiss, Catherine Wolf, David Sennett, Scott Powers, Eric Kraus and Marisa Smith.

INTRODUCTION

When my publisher Eric Kraus first suggested this book to me, I thought, "What a great idea!" But then I wondered "Do that many part-time, show business related jobs really exist? And if they do, will I be able to find them?"

Well, I'm glad to report that after over 250 interviews, a lot of phone calls, and a lot of looking around, I've discovered that not only do they exist, but many are fascinating and well paying (How does $2,500 plus pension and welfare for five hours work, once a week, compare to that waiting job?).

For as long as I can remember, actors have had to go from one "wait" job to another, be bored for hours in front of computer terminals or be stuck on phones trying to sell this or that to totally disinterested strangers. I hope for many of you this book will be the light out of that tunnel. What I discovered during my research was the wealth of different jobs that were somehow connected to one aspect or another of show business.

I really must express my gratitude to the many people who returned phone calls, made themselves available to be interviewed, and were genuinely unselfish enough to be part of a book. I believe this will be an important source book for all actors, dancers, singers, models and performance artists. I trust this book will help you find that "gotta-get-a-job" job as you wait for that lucky break.

Glenn Alterman.

the
JOB BOOK

100 *Acting Jobs*

For Actors

Theatre Refreshments Operations Manager

Notes

Theatre Refreshments Operations Manager

Low Down

The operations manager for theater refreshments is responsible for running theater concessions (including the show merchandising concession). He (or she) must hire and train bartenders as well as all the other staff and on occasion must travel to other theaters in the chain to open their concessions. He handles delivery, technical problems, and shipments, checks weekly concession reports, etc.

Scratch

$400-$700 per week.

Be
- Equipped with managerial skills
- Able to spot trouble and handle it (sometimes very quietly)
- Comfortable and enjoy a theater environment

Perks
- If you're working for a Broadway theater you get to see Broadway shows
- You meet the actors in the shows
- Travel expenses are paid
- Health insurance and paid vacation
- Occasional bonuses
- Employers are "actor-friendly." If you have an audition or get a job, they'll let you out for as long as you need and then allow you to return

Bummers
- You can't be everyone's friend. Sometimes you have to fire another actor
- This can be very time consuming work: 40-50 hours a week
- This job involves a lot of paper work
- Some of this work – such as checking all the shipments, handling deliveries, etc. – can be tedious

Horse's Mouth

Wallace Woods, an actor who's been a Broadway theater refreshments operations manager on and off for 15 years: *"For me, just being in a theater every night, seeing shows, and meeting actors is a big plus. Going to opening nights and being part of live theater on Broadway are just some of the reasons I enjoy this work."*

Contact

Talk to individual theater owners or theater chain owners or check the trades for ads

Eligible Performers
Audition Monitor

Notes

Eligible Performers
Audition Monitor

Low Down
Actors Equity classifies this type of work as "a service." The eligible performers audition monitor runs the Equity auditions. Duties include checking all Equity cards, setting up the appointments for the actors, and handling any problems that may occur.

Scratch
$30 "reimbursement payment" (1099 form).

Be
- Graduate of a two hour class given by Actors Equity
- Competent, reliable, and organized
- Friendly and cheerful
- Cool under pressure and able to deal with actors temperaments

Perks
- You get to meet directors and casting directors
- This is a good way to network with other actors
- You get to serve your fellow actors

Bummers
- Actors' needs can be wearisome
- When a call is for 100 actors and 200 show up
- A long work day (9 hours) for a little money
- There are tension-filled incidents you have to deal with
- The auditioning actors may blame you for failure

Horse's Mouth
Steven Drucker, an actor who has been a monitor several times: *"You don't do it for the money! For me it's about being part of the creative process. Also I've made some good contacts and made good friends."*

Contact
Actors Equity: (212) 869-8530

Buskers:
Street Entertainers

Notes

Contact

There is no one to contact here except your audience. You are your
own boss. Take your act to the streets and good luck!

Buskers:
Street Entertainers

Low Down
If you do acrobatics, sing, break dance, do magic, juggle, whatever, hit the streets my friend. New York, Seattle and San Francisco are "busker-friendly cities." Broadway buskers find out the times a show breaks for intermission and break into their routine as the folks hit the street. With a canister for collecting tips at your side, you can entertain to your heart's delight. Remember, it's only 20 minutes, so make sure they're your best. You may be able to do two intermissions in one night. Don't forget the matinees!

Scratch
Varies widely, depending on the location, the night, the weather, the crowd, etc. Averages $5-$40 per 20 minute shift at intermissions.

Be
- Good at whatever you're doing out there
- Able to keep the crowds attention
- Sure your "show persona" is pleasant and agreeable
- Equipped with a small sound system with a mike if you don't have a strong voice (good breath support)
- Armed with a "gimmick," something to catch their attention
- Endowed with stamina, "chutzpa"
- Prepared – this is your "mini-production", don't waste a moment

Perks
- It's a quick way to make money
- If you're good, the money can be substantial
- You can do a routine on the street that you couldn't do anywhere else
- You are your own boss
- Agents, casting directors, talent scouts all go to the theater.

Bummers
- The weather can be bad
- City noise and traffic can be distracting
- You may have to deal with hecklers and drunks, not to mention crazies
- Your routine may not be appropriate for a specific show's intermission
- You never know how much you'll make from night to night

Horse's Mouth
Tracey Berg, an actress who has been a busker for several years:
"There's nothing like the 'instant on' when that crowd walks out the theater doors. It's also nice to get the bucks right after you've done your work."

Mock Deposition/ Hearing Participant

Notes

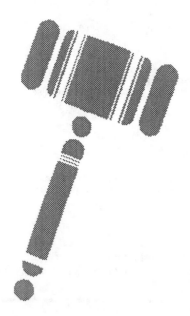

Mock Deposition/ Hearing Participant

Low Down
Actors are hired by law firms and law schools to play witnesses or defendants in mock trials. The junior associates in the firm or law students play the lawyers. This is improv work. You are there to help them hone their skills. You may be directed to be "hostile" or "withholding," depending on the needs of the case. You must be adaptable since they may ask you to change at any point. You are required to learn the "file" for each specific case and then improvise the character.

Scratch
Varies: about $40 an hour.

Be
- Fully grounded in improv work
- Able to turn file material into a living, breathing character
- Adaptable, able to change character moods
- Professional and dress appropriately
- Comfortable in front of a video camera: sometimes they record the trials

Perks
- The work can be very interesting
- You get to hone your improv skills
- Actors are treated well on these jobs
- Your commitment is minimal. You do the job and you're out

Bummers
- These jobs are limited and aren't advertised: you have to pursue them yourself
- The files may be difficult for you to understand

Horse's Mouth
James Prendergast, an actor who has been doing this work for several years: *"This kind of work really keeps you on your toes. It's a great acting exercise and you're treated very well."*

Contact
Check out the individual law schools. In New York, try contacting Heather McMeer at Hofstra. Tel. (516) 463-5916.

Supernumerary
(Extras) For Operas

Notes

Supernumerary
(Extras) For Operas

Low Down

Supernumeraries are hired by individual opera companies to participate, on stage, in the various operas that season. Although once thought of as only "sword carriers," "supers" sometimes have character names in the operas, have specific activities on stage, and are very much part of the dramatic action of the show. An opera like *Aida* may need as many as 230 supernumeraries.

Scratch

Varies, depending on the opera company, the city, etc. Generally, $5-$10 an hour.

Be
- Reliable and have flexible hours for rehearsals
- Able to fit into the costumes they have

Perks
- You get to work in some of the world's greatest operas
- You get on-stage experience before a live audience
- You have the chance to work with great directors
- You may be a "featured super". In the last act of *Tosca*, the Sergeant Executioner and Roberti, two characters in the opera, are actually supers
- In some shows, the supers do more than the chorus

Bummers
- The work is seasonal
- You must have flexible hours
- You receive little pay for sometimes long hours of tedious work
- If you're not an opera fan, this work can sometimes be a bore

Horse's Mouth

John Cole, who hires supers for City Opera in New York:
"Supers can be a significant part of the production. They have the opportunity to work with some of the great directors. And where else, while just doing your job, do you get to hear some of the greatest music ever created?"

Contact

In New York, the Metropolitan Opera Tel. (212) 769-7000 or City Opera Tel. (212) 870-4266 (City Center of Music and Drama.)

Disco Shill

Notes

Disco Shill

Low Down

Some discos and clubs hire attractive, "hot looking" couples to dance when the club opens each night. The purpose is to "get the energy going," "break the ice".

Scratch

Varies, depending on the club. Generally $10-$15 an hour plus free drinks, in moderation, for a four hour shift.

Be
- Attractive, trendy, and comfortable in the club scene
- A good dancer; you don't have to be great
- Friendly, outgoing
- Dressed trendily

Perks
- You get to go to great clubs
- You have a paid night life
- Often, you have a whole dance floor to yourself
- The shifts are short (only four hours), so you can still go out later

Bummers
- This work can get very tiring on a nightly basis
- Late hours can conflict with actors' auditions
- Constant cleaning wears out your wardrobe

Horse's Mouth

Julio Vendez, an actor who occasionally does this work: *"It's one of the great fun gigs. You get paid to party!"*

Contact

Contact clubs to see if they are hiring

Wild West City

Notes

Wild West City

Low Down

If you like playing cowboys, working outdoors, working with horses, entertaining families, this may be the job for you. It's good-guys-bad-guys stuff, make believe holdups, and the pony express. And it all takes place in New Jersey.

Scratch

Varies, depending on the job and your experience. Starts at minimum wage.

Be
- Experienced in stunt work
- Comfortable around horses
- Happy working with the public, especially kids
- In good shape
- Able to do the Can-Can if you're a woman

Perks
- This is fun work
- Entertaining children is satisfying
- You start out in the holdup gang and can work your way up to being the good guy

Bummers
- The money isn't great
- The work is in New Jersey, not New York—difficult to get to auditions
- With stunt work, there is always a possibility of injury

Horse's Mouth

The contact person at Wild West City: *"The actors who work at WWC all seem to enjoy being here a lot. It becomes like one big family every summer. We look for people who are friendly and outgoing. But mostly you've got to like kids to work here."*

Contact

Wild West City, P.O. Box 37, Route 206, Netcong, New Jersey 07857; tel. (201) 347-8900.

Singer For
Choirs Unlimited

Notes

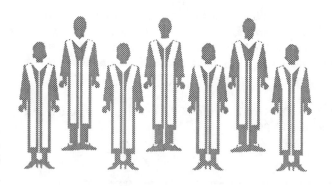

Singer For
Choirs Unlimited

Low Down
Choirs unlimited hires singers and places them in church and synagogue choirs all around the country. Leon Burger, who is a Cantor, created this organization thirty years ago, and still runs it.

Scratch
$50-$100 per service.

Be
- Able to read music (sight reading is a plus)
- Possessed of a well-trained voice
- Comfortable singing in a choir
- Dependable and have flexible hours for rehearsing
- A quick study

Perks
- You get to sing beautiful music
- Travel: Choirs Unlimited places people in choirs all around the country
- There is a lot of this work
- This is a wonderful job for the person who enjoys being in churches and/or synagogues and getting paid

Bummers
- There may be a lot of rehearsal time necessary
- This kind of singing is not for all singers
- They are not interested in Broadway singers. They cannot allow time out of rehearsals for your auditions

Horse's Mouth
Leon Burger, the creator of Choirs Unlimited: *"Basically I'm looking for good, loyal choir singers. I hire for everyone from Seventh Day Adventists to major Jewish Synagogues all around the country. If you feel this is the kind of work for you, please don't hesitate to call."*

Contact
Leon Burger, 2404 Ocean Avenue, Brooklyn, New York 11229; telephone: (718) 934-3252.

Doctor-Patient Simulation

Notes

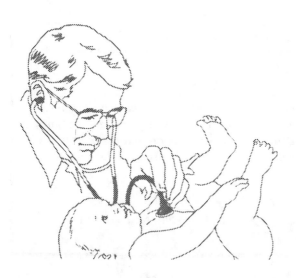

Doctor-Patient Simulation

Low Down
Actors assist medical students in improvisational doctor-patient situations. It is necessary to learn a patient's medical history and be able to act the symptoms out for the doctor. Diseases range from Alcoholism to Alzheimers. The average work period is five or six weeks. This work is intended to help future doctors improve their "bedside manner."

Scratch
$10-$14 an hour.

Be
- Possessed of excellent improv skills
- Adaptable, take directions well
- Able to understand the patient's history and turn it into actable behavior

Perks
- You get to hone your improv skills
- You'll get some insights into medical protocol
- You don't have to make a long commitment

Bummers
- There's not much of this work around
- You must be able to understand material that at times can be very complex

Horse's Mouth
Laura Patenkin, an actress who has done this work: *"I feel this work helped build a confidence in my acting skills. Acting with doctors, who are non-actors, makes you work twice as hard. I only wish there was more of this work."*

Contact
Hospitals and medicals schools in your area.

Night Club Act Creator And Coach

Notes

Night Club Act Creator And Coach

Low Down
You help performers develop a concept and style for their night club (cabaret) act. You help with the selection of songs, development of the patter between songs, the interpretation of the songs (including delivery), and all other aspects of the act.

Scratch
Varies, averages $40-$50 an hour.

Be
- A good organizer
- Able to work well with all kinds of performers
- Knowledgeable in all aspects of cabaret performance, right down to lighting and sound systems
- Perceptive and sensitive to the needs of the performers and what they're trying to say in their act
- Knowledgeable in all aspects of public relations for this kind of work: selecting the right head shots, knowing how to do a press kit, etc.
- Experienced, having had your own cabaret act is helpful
- Tasteful and know all types of material

Perks
- The money can be very good
- It's a very creative job
- Developing and then seeing a good act by another performer can be satisfying
- By helping develop other acts, you may discover some secrets, tricks, etc. that will be useful in your own act

Bummers
- Some performers' emotional trips can be very exhausting
- Sometimes the talent you're working with isn't so talented
- Not being able to find the right concept or material for a specific performer can be frustrating

Horse's Mouth
Margery Beddow, an actress who has been coaching night club acts for nearly ten years: *"It's really about trying to discover what it is the performer is trying to say. The clearer they can be the more you can be in helping them express themselves."*

Contact
Most of this work is word-of-mouth. Place an ad in a trade paper.

Using Your Pets In The Business

Notes

Contact
All Tame Animals, 457 West 57th Street, New York, NY 10019.
Speak to Barbara Weir; tel. (212) 245-6740 or try Antelope to
Zebra Agency, 19 Indian Trail, Sparta, New Jersey, 07871. tel.
(201) 729-8442.

Using Your Pets In The Business

Low Down

In this field you can use your pet to make money. If your cat has a "special look" and is *very* easygoing around people, then there might be some money in it for you. Dogs must have obedience training, be able to take commands, have a special or unusual look, and be comfortable around a lot of people. The work here is in television, film, and print.

Scratch

Varies: anywhere from $100-$800 per day.

Be
- Dogs must have obedience training. Generally, obedience schools cost $200 and up
- Cats must have a very low key temperament and be comfortable in high pressure situations
- Animals must be photographed, like head shots for actors
- You must train your dogs on an ongoing basis. Also, depending on the job, there are always new tricks to be taught
- You must register your animal with animal talent agents

Perks
- If your animal becomes successful in this field, you can negotiate high fees
- Seeing your pet on television, on film, or in print

Bummers
- Pets can be overworked. You must protect your pet. Quite often they won't get a break on a set unless you ask for it
- You constantly have to teach your pet new tricks
- There are initial expenses: head shots for the pet, obedience schools, etc

Horse's Mouth

Judy Jensen, an actress who has a pet actor, her dog: *"Your animal must really enjoy this kind of work; you can't force it on him. You must protect your animal, make sure he's given breaks and isn't overworked."*

Talking Book Recorder

Notes

Talking Book Recorder

Low Down
You record entire books (some abridged) onto tapes that are later made into cassettes. It should sound like you're "reading to your blind grandmother."

Scratch
$45-$65 an hour.

Be
- Able to enunciate in neutral American speech. Canadian speech is also desirable
- Pleasant-sounding
- Able to control your vocal dynamic range: make your voice more intense rather than scream; maintain a soft sound without whispering
- Possessed of perfect diction

Perks
- The money is good
- There is a lot of this work
- Once you understand the technique it can be very pleasant work
- You'll get to read some wonderful books
- You only work when you're available

Horse's Mouth
Anthony Henderson, who casts actors for this kind of work:
"Talking books is either a skill you have or you don't. It's amazing how many actors I listen to who have bad speech and pronunciation. If you're right for this kind of work it can be a very pleasant way to earn a living."

Contact
American Printing House For The Blind, Louisville, Kentucky; Talking Books, Denver, Colorado, or most major publishers' talking books departments

Piano
Accompanist

Notes

Piano Accompanist

Low Down
Accompany singers at auditions, in rehearsals, in coaching, in cabaret acts.

Scratch
$25-$75 an hour.

Be
- Able to sight read music
- Able to listen to what the singer is doing
- Able to know the difference between just what's on the page and what the song is about
- Adaptable, flexible, able to work with all kinds of singers
- Able to play many different styles

Perks
- This work can be a satisfying challenge
- You can help make a singer sound good
- If you enjoy playing piano, it's a wonderful way to make a living
- Can be a venue for other work

Bummers
- You lack job security. You never know when you'll be working
- Quite often at auditions the pianos are out of tune. You have to deal with it
- The accompanist can be blamed for failed auditions if singers forget lyrics, jump lines, etc
- Sometimes you're thrown into the role of shrink or father to some singers
- You must continuously buy new material to keep up with the latest scores

Horse's Mouth
John Delfin, a piano accompanist for 14 years: *"I find this kind of work very challenging. You can turn craft into art. Each person you accompany has a different way of working. Part of the job is finding the best way to work with them."*

Contact
Much of this work is word-of-mouth. Advertise in the trades.

Cruise Ship

Notes

Contact

The "entertainment packages" of most cruise ships are created by the booking agents that the cruises hire. Cruise ships may work with only one or several booking agents. To find work on cruise ships, you should contact the cruise agents or a producer who books these cruises. Here are a few:

- Alford Productions
  PABT, Box 21029
  New York, NY 10129-0009
  (Casting director: Ted Hook)

- Jean Ann Ryan Productions
  308 S.E. 14th Street
  Fort Lauderdale, FL 33316
  (Contact: Jean Ann Ryan)

- Bramson Entertainment Bureau
  1440 Broadway
  New York, NY 10018
  (Contact: James Abramson)

- G&C Entertainment
  Box 1603
  Ansonia Station,
  New York, NY 10023

Cruise Ship

Low Down
Cruise ships hire three types of performers: musical revues – 45 to 60 minutes, 5 to 10 performers; book musicals: this is a "condensed musical" (usually a Broadway show); individual acts: anything from a comedian to a magician. Aside from actual performing work one may be expected to be part of the cruise staff: work in the ship's library, run bingo games, and socialize with passengers. Usually you are hired for a six month stint. But specific ship cruises may only be one day to three months.

Scratch
Varies widely: $250-$500 a week for musical revues and show girls; $350-$550 a week for book musical performers; $250-$1,500 for individual acts.

Be
- Aside from your specific performing skill, there isn't much else required

Perks
- Exotic paid vacations
- You are part of a huge family at sea
- The food and services on most cruise ships are excellent
- Cruise ship entertainers make life-long friendships on cruises

Bummers
- Sea sickness
- You have to socialize with passengers even if you're not feeling up to it
- You may be asked to do other crew work you don't want to do such as bingo games
- Committments for up to six months; this can lock you into being away from family, friends, and other work

Horse's Mouth
Larry Reese, a singer who has been doing cruise ships for seven years: "*It is probably the most enjoyable kind of work I've ever done. You make friendships with some of the most interesting people in the world. The actual work is relatively easy and you're not under the pressure of critics or reviews. People on cruises 'want' to enjoy you. They're there just to have fun.*"

Theatre Ticket Broker at Hotels

Notes

Theatre Ticket Broker at Hotels

Low Down
Theater ticket brokers work in selling booths at various hotels. Their job is to help visitors select a show (Broadway or Off-Broadway) based on the visitors' entertainment preferences. Part of the job is to also help the out-of-towner find the best route to the show.

Scratch
$9 an hour and up. You can also work full-time on a commission versus advance basis.

Be
- Knowledgeable about the shows that you're recommending.
- Neat looking, a self-starter
- Polite, confident
- Prepared: most companies train you for up to two months for this work

Perks
- Meet all kinds of people
- Quite often different shows comp ticket brokers to their shows so they'll recommend them
- The employer is actor friendly and will work with you if you have an audition or get a job
- If you work on a commission basis, this work can be very lucrative
- The hours are flexible

Bummers
- Some customers are irritating or indecisive
- Customers may have problems after tickets are purchased
- Usually you work alone, which can be boring if you're not busy

Horse's Mouth
Alan Moore, owner of Continental Guest Services, the largest ticket broker in New York: *"We like to work mainly with actors because they know the most about the shows we sell and they're generally outgoing and friendly"*

Contact
Continental Guest Services, 1501 Broadway – Room 1814, New York, NY 10036.

Santa Claus

Notes

Santa Claus

Low Down

Here's the chance to play everyone's favorite Christmas giftgiver. There is work in malls, at Macy's, and at private parties.

Scratch

Varies, depending on location. $7-$13 and hour in department stores and malls. Up to $50 an hour for private and corporate parties.

Be
- In love with all children
- Able to say "Ho-ho-ho!" with heartfelt sincerity a million times in one day
- Able to show composure under pressure: the average "Santa visit" is under 30 seconds, but you must make the little one's believe they're having a long visit.
- Patient – it's a required virtue in this work

Perks
- Making a little kid believe in Santa Clause is satisfying
- You can make good money, and big tips at corporate parties
- This can be really fun work

Bummers
- In malls you may work eight hours with only a half hour to one hour lunch break.
- Each Santa operation has its own rules
- If you want to buy your own Santa suit it can run you up to $1,000. The average suit is a few hundred dollars
- You may have to work under hot lights wearing an outdoor costume indoors
- Kids may have colds which you'll catch, putting you out of commission
- The glue to hold the beard on can irritate your skin

Horse's Mouth

David Sennet, an actor who has been playing Santa for years: *"There is no job that gives me more joy than playing Santa at Macy's. I wish everyone could see the children's faces. If they did, I'm sure there'd be a million more Santas at Christmas."*

Contact

Macy's, Tel. (212) 695-5440, and other department stores as well as Western Temp hires Santas.

Club Kid

Notes

Club Kid

Low Down
In some ways this may be the easiest job of all. Basically all you have to do is show up at the club and be "fabulous". Popular members of the "club scene" are paid a nice fee just to frequent certain clubs. The notoriety of the "club kid" determines how much he/she will get. Usually these are the most outrageous and popular kids in town. Some club-kids-for-hire work two or three clubs a night. Just their being there makes the club a more "in" place.

Scratch
Varies: up to $250 a night.

Be
- Equipped with a creative, outrageous taste in make-up, wardrobe, style
- Seen hanging out where the action is
- There and "work it." There is no way to predict who will become the top in a world of outrageous style.

Perks
- You're paid to do what you used to do for nothing
- You get to meet the hottest people in the club scene
- You're usually given free drinks
- You have proof that you really are a "star"
- This kind of exposure can lead to cabaret, film, and television work

Bummers
- You have to put in late nights
- Your wardrobe needs to be constantly updated since you are constantly "re-inventing" yourself

Horse's Mouth
Miss Bobby-Dee, one of New York's club kids: *"What can I say? You get to go out, see your friends, have fun, and put a couple of bucks away. What could be better?"*

Contact
There is no one to contact, just places to go. You have to find the latest trendy club and be part of the scene there. Usually the owners will contact you. It's a no-rules business.

Police Crisis-Intervention Trainer

Notes

Police Crisis-Intervention Trainer

Low Down
In this type of simulation work you are hired by police stations or police academies to act out certain crisis-intervention scenarios. The most common situations are suicide and domestic violence. Quite often you are asked to create the situation. Each scenario is ten to fifteen minutes.

Scratch
$10-$15 an hour

Be
- Very experienced in improv work
- Comfortable in intense, realistic, sometimes depressing, on-the-edge scenarios
- Imaginative: a healthy imagination is a real plus

Perks
- The work can be fascinating
- Knowing that you are helping to prevent future crimes and may someday save a life is rewarding
- You only work four to five hours, so you still have time to go to auditions
- You get a great deal of experience learning to trust other actors in intense acting situations

Bummers
- The work is sporadic
- You have to find this work; it's not advertised
- If you're not careful, the volatile situations can be dangerous

Horse's Mouth
Richard Springle, an actor who has done this work: *"I found it to be incredible freeing. You really get to test your mettle, see how far you can go. The intense situations are exciting to play."*

Contact
Nearby police stations, police academies, and criminal training schools.

Stilt Walker

Notes

Stilt Walker

Low Down

There are two kinds of stilts. "Painter stilts" are two long sticks, one with a toe and one with a heel. These are mostly used when painting or when doing promotion work where walking isn't too important. "Peg stilts" are long poles that give the walker more flexibility and versatility. Stilt walkers are used in parades, at parties, at concerts, and for all sorts of promotional work. They are in great demand in Las Vegas.

Scratch

$75-$125 an hour

Be
- Possessed of tremendous balance
- Well-trained: you can get up on stilts in a day or two, but it takes about six months until you're comfortable with them. Learning the "variations" you can do with stilts may take up to a year

Perks
- Once you've mastered it, it can be great fun
- The feeling of being so high above people is an odd pleasure
- You get to work incredible parties and events that normally you never would have been invited to
- You can travel to wonderful places

Bummers
- It can be very tiresome
- Yes, you can fall, and there is little you can do to protect yourself

Horse's Mouth

Ken Romo, a dancer who has been stilt-walking for many years: *"I can't begin to tell you how incredible it feels to be up there. It's the kind of work that exists no where else. The looks in people's faces, the smiles, are incredible."*

Contact

Talk to entertainment and party agents and let them know you're available. Place ads in magazines.

Improv Group

Notes

Improv Group

Low Down

Improv work includes no script. As a group you take suggestions from the audience on specific topics such as current events, or politics, and then act them out. This kind of work is totally spontaneous. Every night a different show.

Scratch

About $125 per show in a good improv group like Chicago City Limits.

Be
- Possessed of good listening skills
- Able to play off your fellow actor without censoring
- Able to trust your fellow actor
- Comfortable with your own body
- Up-to-date on current events
- Funny: comedic timing is a plus, but it's not mandatory
- Strong in improv techniques

Perks
- You work steadily
- You get constant exposure
- Often, there is a family atmosphere in the company
- You get to use all your performing skills: singing, dancing, etc.

Bummers
- Improv work is not very "saleable" in the performing arts. It's considered the "underworld" in show business
- It can be physically exhausting
- Sometimes it's difficult to find your "niche" in the group, that which makes you different from the other actors
- Hecklers and audience members sometimes want "lewd" improvs
- Sometimes people in the audience compete with the group on stage
- Some nights you don't have good shows, which can be depressing

Horse's Mouth

Alison Grambs, a working member of the improv group Chicago City Limits: *"There is something incredibly rewarding about bringing a character to life on the spot. You use yourself completely in this work, and learn to rely on all your performing skills".*

Contact

Chicago City Limits tel. (212) 772-8707, Gotham City Improv tel. (212) 714-1477 or any of the smaller improv groups springing up.

Corporate Speaker Consultant

Notes

Corporate Speaker Consultant

Low Down

In this field you work with everyone from corporate sales managers up to corporate vice presidents. You train them to present themselves attractively and to be entertaining at speeches and meetings. Some of the material can be very dull (called "info dump"); you have to devise a way to make it interesting.

Scratch

Vary: generally about $40-$50 an hour, or $300 a day plus expenses.

Be
- Tremendously concentrated and able to talk about material you don't know
- Articulate and have a good vocabulary
- Professional: you're dealing with successful business people (Ph.D.'s and M.B.A.'s), it's important that you behave appropriately

Perks
- You make very good money for very little work: usually three to four hours a day
- World-wide travel
- You meet the movers and shakers in big business

Bummers
- You are constantly being scrutinized by the people you're working with and for
- Most work is out-of-town, taking you away from possible acting work

Horse's Mouth

David Sennett, an actor who does speaker consulting: *"This kind of work allows me to combine my directing, teaching, and acting skills. The thing that is most exciting about this work is that the stakes are high and for real."*

Contact

There are people who specifically sub-contract this work. Call the human resources, public relations, or marketing department at any major company to inquire.

Walk-Around
Costume Character

Notes

Walk-Around Costume Character

Low Down

You are hired by stores (*e.g.* F.A.O. Schwartz, Warner Brothers stores) to walk around dressed as a specific cartoon character or toy. For Warner Brothers you may be Tweety Bird or Sylvester, for F.A.O. Schwartz you may be Raggedy Ann. You walk around the store (in character) and greet children, sign autographs, and just play. In the stores you generally have a five hour shift.

Scratch

Vary: $10-$12 an hour for a minimum of four hours in stores; $25 an hour for private parties.

Be
- Totally in love with children
- Comfortable acting silly
- Able to maintain a character for up to five hours

Perks
- The work is fun
- If you love kids, this is the job for you
- You get to meet a lot of celebrities and their kids
- This work can be very lucrative if you get into the children's party circuit

Bummers
- You're on your feet for five hours
- The wig hair from the costumes is very unflattering to your own hair: It flattens your hair and makes you look unkempt. This can be trouble if you have an audition right after work
- Teen-agers can be mean pranksters
- Your costume and wig may frighten young children.

Horse's Mouth

Barbara Flynn, an actress who has been doing this work for several years: *"This is one of the most delightful jobs I've ever head. I get to play with children, have fun, and just be silly every day."*

Contact

F.A.O. Schwartz tel. (212) 644-9400; Warner Brothers stores tel. (212) 754-0300, and entertainment and party talent agents.

Medieval Times Performer

Notes

Contact

Medieval Times, 149 Polito ave, Lindhurst, New Jersey, 07071; tel. (800) 828-2945.

Medieval Times Performer

Low Down

If you like jousting, sword fighting, horseback riding, and athletics, this may be the job for you. As the name implies the theme is medieval. There are wenches and squires, fair ladies and all the rest. The families come to be entertained and enjoy all the majesty and splendor of a medieval fair combined with a good old fashioned feast, all in two hours.

Scratch

Vary: up to $15 an hour for Squires/Knights, $50-$120 for three hour shift for waitpersons.

Be

(*For squires/knights:*)
- Very athletic
- Possessed of swordfighting skills
- Well trained with horses/able to joust
- Squires are trained for six months to become knights

(*For wenches/serfs (waitpersons)*)
- Comfortable in a noisy, very active hall
- Able to maintain medieval character while serving food

(*For Squires/Knights and Wenches*)
- Happy working with people, especially kids

Perks

- A lot of fun
- The work is exciting and each show is different
- You work from about four until ten p.m., so you can get to auditions and still not work late hours
- There is a camaraderie among workers; the crew becomes like a family

Bummers

- Knights can get hurt by horses, swords, etc.
- The work can be grueling: some days there are three shows

Horse's Mouth

Laurie Rovtar Piro, an administrator at Medieval Times: *"The show is timed beautifully. From marketing to performing you'll find it a fun place to work. We try to treat our people well."*

Roger Mazzeo, an actor who has worked at Medieval Times: *"The time flies by. It's a wonderful way to entertain people."*

Looping or Group Looping Artist

Notes

Contact
Finding looping work can be difficult, but once found can be lucrative. The Screen Actors Guild, tel. (212) 944-1030, occasionally lists loop groups. Also, try the Working Actors Guide. Other than that it's just word of mouth and finding out who's looking.

Looping or Group Looping Artist

Low Down
Also known as ADR (Automatic Dialogue Replacement), looping is putting additional sounds on movies or television shows. This includes anything from a few lines to generalized "atmosphere." "Group looping" occurs when groups of actors do this work. Group looping is more prevalent in Hollywood than New York. Sometimes actors "re-voice" a small character in the movie. Looping of a movie is done in small sections.

Scratch
Varies, depending on work required. Screen Actors Guild rate is $504 a day.

Be
- Able to improvise, think on your feet, ad lib
- Able to do relaxed, moment-to-moment work
- Able to perform different accents and younger and older voices

Perks
- This can be fun, challenging work
- In Los Angeles, if you get hooked up with some good groups, it can be very lucrative

Bummers
- Sometimes you work with other actors in the group who are untrained, which can be very frustrating
- Most of this work is in Los Angeles
- Getting connected with a good group can be difficult

Horse's Mouth
Richard Kennerton, an actor who has done group looping in Los Angeles: *"I find the work very challenging. When I was hooked up with a couple of groups in Los Angeles I was making very good money and had work on an ongoing basis. As to actual work, I found that whenever I was in public places I'd listen to how and what people talked about. I jotted down "key phrases" that I'd later include in my loops."*

Theater Concession Sales Attendant

Notes

Contact
Wallace Woods or Julian Rubin c/o Theater Refreshments, 346 West 44th Street, New York, NY 10036; tel. (212) 586-7610.

Theater Concession Sales Attendant

Low Down

This is bartending work or merchandising concessions work at theaters. The bartenders are responsible for setting up the bar, and then serving alcohol, soda, and candy to the audience before the show and at intermission. The merchandising concession person displays the materials and sells before the show, at intermission, and after the show.

Scratch

$14-$25 per shift, plus $10-$40 per shift in tips

Be
- Friendly, outgoing, and polite
- Neat and able to organize stock well
- Happy working in a theater
- One employer says he only hires dependable and efficient workers who can break down a bar in less than three minutes (after intermission)
- Bartenders are trained for two weeks and hired on a trial basis for six weeks

Perks
- You get to work in a Broadway theater and see the show as often as you like
- Employers will work around actors' schedules (auditions, acting jobs, etc.)
- You can work at theaters in Los Angeles
- You develop close friendships with the other workers
- The hours are short, and the work is not too difficult

Bummers
- You have to deal with irate customers
- Some nights you won't make enough tips
- Your evenings are tied up

Horse's Mouth

Wallace Woods, who hires actors for these jobs: *"It's really an ideal bread and butter job for an actor. The hours aren't long, and the work isn't really hard. It's a pleasant way to make a buck in the business."*

Radio Disc Jockey

Notes

Contact

Contact specific radio stations to see who is hiring. The smaller, more out of the way stations (who usually pay less) are your best shot. Also check out AFTRA (American Federation of Television and Radio Artists) tel. (212) 532-0800, publications and bulletin boards.

Radio Disc Jockey

Low Down
The work of the DJ on a show depends on the show's format (soft music, topical issues, etc.). DJ's on the smaller radio stations are expected to do other jobs along with their on-air duties. They may be expected to write commercial copy, sell ads, and in some cases even operate the transmitter.

Scratch
Union DJ's: Morning DJ's average $85,000, midday $40,000, afternoon $50,000, evening $33,000, and overnight DJ's $25,000. Non-union DJ's: $5-$20 an hour.

Be
- Able to think on your feet
- Equipped with a pleasant and interesting voice, including good diction, vocabulary and pronunciation
- Aware of current events
- Skillful at writing for news and commercials
  (*College is a plus*)

Perks
- If you critique movies and shows you are given free tickets
- On occasion you receive freebies, although most of that ended with "Payola"
- DJ's are local celebrities
- A good venue for exposure, which can lead to better jobs in the show business
- You are using some of your talent

Bummers
- Off-air duties can get time consuming
- Anything can go wrong on the air
- You have very little job security
- When starting out, you may get the worst shift
- Working live can be very stressful

Horse's Mouth
Sam Zema, who has worked on several small radio stations as a DJ: *"I found the work challenging. When you work a call-in show you never know who will be on the other end of the line and what they'll say. It certainly keeps you on your toes!"*

Singing Waiter

Notes

Singing Waiter

Low Down
Singing waitering is a wonderful way for the singer to earn extra money. It provides the opportunity to perform before a live audience on a nightly basis. As a rule, waitresses take the orders, serve the food, and that's it. They never go into the kitchen; the food is brought out for them to serve. While waiting for the order, the waitress has time to sing one song. Each waitress sings about one song an hour.

Scratch
Varies, averaging $50-$150 a night.

Be
- A well trained singer with a good voice
- Equipped with good waitering skills. The point of this kind of work is that you're able to go up on the stage and sing and not be preoccupied with the people at your tables.

Perks
- You sing every night before a live audience
- You try out new songs
- It's a showcase situation where talent scouts and agents can check out your work
- Most restaurant owners are "talent-friendly" and flexible to the needs of singers and actors. If you get a job you're usually welcomed back when you're in town again

Horse's Mouth
Billy Grey, owner of the Gaslight Club, a restaurant that hires singing waitresses: *"For some singers this is the perfect bread and butter job. We try to give them every opportunity to showcase their talent every night."*

Contact
Billy Grey, The Gaslight Club, Hotel Dorset, New York City. Trade papers usually list casting for singing waiter/waitress work

Strip-O-Gram

Notes

Strip-O-Gram

Low Down
If you have a nice body, enjoy people and parties, and aren't modest, this may be the work for you. Models who do strip-o-grams are assigned parties, show up dressed, and then with some fantasy pretext (*e.g.* police officer, woman in a cake) begin to playfully undress for the party guests. The average job is about 20 minutes.

Scratch
Varies: can be up to $250 a night.

Be
- In excellent shape and able to move well
- Outgoing; like to play and have fun
- Able to forget modesty
- Able to convince the party guests that you've come for another reason and then spring the surprise strip on them

Perks
- You can make quick, easy money: $40-$50 for 20 minutes
- The work is fun
- This is an exhibitionist's dream
- The best bodies work the most
- The work is steady
- You can do up to five jobs in one night

Bummers
- Party guests can hit on you
- Your schedule is uncertain: you're always on call
- You never know what the next part will be like
- You have to be careful not to strip in a lewd manner

Horse's Mouth
Bret Morgan, who hires models for Hardbodies, Inc. in New York:
"There's no doubt that the best bodies work the most, that more women work than men (two to one), and that it can be a real fun job. You don't have to be a professional stripper or dancer to do this kind of work. If you feel you'd like to try it please give us a call."

Contact
Hardbodies, Inc: (212) 988-4888, (516) 328-6700, (718) 693-9441. Other strip-o-gram agencies are listed in *New York Magazine*, and *The Village Voice*.

Warm Up for Television Shows

Notes

Horse's Mouth
Wendee Cole, who's done warm-up for nine years, and has worked on such shows as *Mad About You*, *Designing Women*, *Night Court*, *Evening Shade*, and *A Different World*: *"It takes a very special person to do warm-up. It's not as easy as you may think. The secret is in the job title. You have to "warm-up" the audience. You must keep them interested."*

Contact
The best way to find work in this field is to be recommended to a producer of one of the shows. If that's not possible, call the individual shows to see if you can send them a tape of your work (doing stand-up for example) or have them come see you if you're appearing somewhere.

Warm Up for Television Shows

Low Down

The warm-up entertainer's job is to keep television audience (about 250-350 people) entertained, interested, and up-beat. Although having stand-up comedy in your background is helpful, this job relies on many more skills. The warm-up may start off telling jokes but with an average of 15 scenes in a sit-com, the stand up may have to keep the audience occupied for up to ten minutes between each scene (150 minutes). He or she must keep them interested in the story of the show, the characters, etc. Some warm-ups interview audience members, improvise games, or give away prizes. The secret is to give the audience a feeling that they are part of the show, to include them in some way.

Scratch

$500-$2,500, plus pension and welfare, for up to five hours work.

Be
- Possessed of a good sense of humor
- Happy being with people

Perks
- You can make very good money for only a few hours of enjoyable work
- You can make very good contacts
- It's possible to go from warm-up on a show to writer
- Since the hours are short, you have time to pursue other work
- Warm-up work leads to more warm-up work. If you're good, you can work several shows

Bummers
- You may be "type cast" as a warm-up and find it difficult to find other work
- The producers want someone who is funny, but not funnier than the show
- It can be difficult for women to break into this kind of work
- Producers want to see a prospective warm-up's stand-up comedy tapes, which aren't necessarily the best way to tell if you can do this kind of work

Horse's Mouth

Joanne Curley Kerner, producer, *Grace Under Fire:* "*We don't necessarily look for stand-ups for this kind of work. We want people who can keep an audience interested in the show, up-beat, and entertained.*"

Game Show Development Actor

Notes

Game Show Development Actor

Low Down
In this kind of work, actors are hired during the developmental phase of creating a new television game show. The actor may play the role of "contestant", "celebrity", or "host". You're given the rules for the game and all you do is play as best you can. Producers, directors, and backers watch the run through and determine its possibilities.

Scratch
About $10 an hour

Be
- Able to enjoy playing games
- Genuinely friendly and outgoing
- Flexible: you may be called at the last minute
- Able to keep your mouth shut. Some producers look to you for suggestions, others don't

Perks
- The games are usually fun to play
- If you're ambitious, you may get in on the ground level to work as a writer or production assistant on the show
- It's quick, easy money

Bummers
- You may discover, in front of a group of producers, that you're not so bright, and it can be embarrassing.
- If the game show goes on the air, you can't go on as a contestant. It's illegal since you worked with the production team

Horse's Mouth
Louise Keilson, an actress who has done this kind of work: *"I really enjoy this kind of work. You never know what kind of game it'll be, who'll be involved, and where it may take you."*

Contact
The best way to get this kind of work is to contact the individual producers of game shows and let them know that you're interested.

Commercial Print Model

Notes

Contact
There are quite a few model agencies in New York. Call them and
find out when they have open hours or what their submission
policy for new models is.

Commercial Print Model

Low Down

Commercial print models represent the idealized versions of everyday types. These models appear in magazines, in newspapers, and on billboards. They must give the appearance of "truthful behavior in imaginary circumstances."

Scratch

Varies, generally about $250 an hour, $1,000-$2,000 a day.

Be
- Able to portray, and be instantly believable as a specific "type": a daddy, an executive, a mom
- Equipped with "head shots" that show your type in one second
- Equipped with a "composite" that shows a day in the life of your type
- Confident in yourself, pleasant and congenial
- Comfortable in front of the camera
- Able to use your acting skills to create instant believability
- Well groomed: take excellent care of hair, skin and nails

Perks
- This is an excellent way to supplement your acting career
- Print ads may turn into television commercials, which can be very lucrative
- Modeling can be an excellent ego perk
- You can choose when you are available and book out when you're not

Bummers
- There is the possibility of rejection
- You have to attend endless go-sees
- The uncertainty of when you'll book a job creates income uncertainty
- You need an extensive wardrobe
- Head shots and composites are costly

Horse's Mouth

Scott Powers, a commercial print model who runs workshops in New York in this field: *"This is an excellent way for actors to make money. It can be fun, interesting, and a good venue for other work in show business."*

Reader
for Soaps, T.V. & Theater

Notes

Contact

Contact casting directors for individual shows or projects and let them know you are interested in being a reader.

Reader
for Soaps, T.V. & Theater

Low Down
The reader's job is to read opposite actors at auditions. Usually the reader is given the script (sides) in advance. Sometimes as part of his or her job, he welcomes the talent, introduces himself, and tries to make them comfortable. The focus of the reader's work is to make the auditioning actor look good, not to give a stand-out performance himself.

Scratch
Varies, averaging $100 a day for film and television, $50 a day for theater.

Be
- Comfortable within the pressure of an audition situation
- Pleasant and friendly
- Capable of giving a "serviceable" reading of the script without needing to "knock their socks off ".

Perks
- You get to see what works and doesn't work in an audition situation
- You get to meet and work with casting directors, directors, and playwrights

Bummers
- You sometimes have to deal with "actor attitude/hostility".
- Sometimes you read for a role that you know you're right for and yet didn't get to audition for

Horse's Mouth
Albert Proia, an actor who occasionally reads: *"I've learned a great deal from this work about the best ways to conduct yourself at an audition. By watching good actors give a good audition you can pick up a lot of little tips."*

Desktop Publisher
of Flyers, Resumés & Programs

Notes

Contact
This is a "self-start" operation. Once you have all the equipment
you have to let people know that you've set up shop. Try ads in the
trade papers, signs on bulletin boards where actors congregate
and flyers.

Desktop Publisher
of Flyers, Resumés & Programs

Low Down

If you have a good, well-equipped computer and know the basics of art design this may be the work for you. The work includes designing the layouts for resumés, designing flyers, and creating programs for shows.

Scratch

Varies: about $25 a resumé; $30 per hour for flyers.

Be
- Equipped with excellent computer skills
- Know the basics of graphics and have equipment that can do all kinds of constructions
- Have a desktop publishing program
- Have collaborative skills
- Have the capability to articulate and clarify your concepts about a specific design
- Understand the concepts of what points need to be highlighted to make a resumé most effective

Perks
- An excellent way to network with other actors and theaters
- A personal sense of accomplishment when a job is well done
- Since it's your own business, you have flexibility of hours
- It's another creative outlet
- Quite often you get freebies from theaters you're working with

Bummers
- Actors can be indecisive about what they want
- Sometimes you must be available at odd hours
- You must keep up with the rapid changes in computer software

Horse's Mouth

Doug Barron, an actor who is also the owner of Plaza Desk Top Publishing: *"To do this kind of work you really must be more of an art director than a computer person. I recommend that you get an assistant who can cover for you if you get acting work."*

Puppeteer

Notes

Puppeteer

Low Down

There are many kinds of puppets and many places they are used. Puppets are used on television and in film as well in live performance. Educational departments have found that puppets are an effective way to teach everything from English to drug abuse prevention. The puppeteer has many possible venues to choose from when looking for employment.

Scratch

Varies, depending on medium. $350 a day and up for television work.

Be
• Able to develop arm strength
• Flexible with your hands, have dexterity
• Able to develop vocal flexibility
• Able to collaborate well with others in the field
• Able to work with television monitors (everything is backwards)
• Theater training is very helpful
• If you can design puppets it's a plus
• A childrens' theater background is helpful

Perks
• Very gratifying work if you like to work with children
• Travel, sometimes world-wide
• If you get a television show, the money is very good

Bummers
• There can be a lack of work
• This work can be tiring, very demanding
• There are constant time restraints in television work
• Three-camera shoots can be difficult to master
• You almost have to be a contortionist to do some of this work

Horse's Mouth

Robert Gardner, a puppeteer who has worked with the Muppets: *"There is something magical about bringing an inanimate object to life. For me the best part is the look on the children's faces during the show."*

Contact

Start off with the Muppets. Try the children's television network *Nickelodeon* tel. (212) 258-7500. Many children's theater companies use puppets: Finding work is basically a search and find mission for the ambitious puppeteer.

Casting Seminar Creator

Notes

Contact

The only way to begin this work is by setting up appointments with casting directors and talent agents. There is a lot of necessary groundwork and expense before your first seminar.

Casting Seminar Creator

Low Down
In the last few years casting seminars have become one of the most effective ways to meet agents and casting directors. Since they are relatively inexpensive, actors don't mind putting out the $25 or so per session to have their work seen by people who previously they've had no luck in contacting. Bunny Levine, an actress, set up The Actors Connection, one of the most successful seminars in New York, to supplement her income. Several other actors (both in New York and L.A.) have created their own seminars.

Scratch
$5,000-$30,000 a year

Be
- Knowledgeable about casting directors, talent agents, and actors
- Possessed of a genuine empathy for actors
- Able to determine if an actor will be detrimental to the seminar
- Organized. There are schedules to set up, appointments to make
- Able to work well under pressure. Last minute agent cancellations can be very unnerving

Perks
- It can be very gratifying to see actors improve from seminar to seminar
- Seminars are a great way to network
- You get to see a great show every night. The monologues performed by the actors can be very entertaining.
- This work can be lucrative

Bummers
- Casting directors cancel at the last minute, actors cancel
- It can be difficult to have to tell an actor that he needs more study
- The chemistry of each night's group is uncertain
- When first creating a seminar, there are some major expenses: advertising, space rental, and staff
- This work is time consuming: aside from the nightly seminars, a lot of daytime organizational work is involved

Horse's Mouth
Bunny Levine, the actress who created The Actors Connection:
"For all its many problems I still find this work very gratifying. When you see an actor finally succeed after years of trying, and you know that the seminar helped in his success, it's a very rewarding feeling."

Artist's Model

Notes

Artist's Model

Low Down

Artists' models pose, sometimes nude and sometimes partially nude, for groups of artists. Sometimes these models are employed by drawing classes and sometimes by professional artists' groups. The model should be able to remain in a specific pose for up to twenty minutes. After a short break they must be able to return to the prior pose. In sculpture work they should be able to retain these poses, with twenty minutes breaks, for up to three hours.

Scratch
$10-$15 an hour

Be
- Comfortable with nudity and posing
- Able to remain still for up to twenty minutes
- Well rested: you don't want to fall asleep!
- Awareness of how lighting affects your body is helpful

Perks
- You work when you're available
- Seeing yourself in drawings and sculptures is satisfying
- You know that you've helped other artist's in their work

Bummers
- Physical discomfort: you get "pins and needles"
- No union means no benefits
- Posing can make you feel very vulnerable
- You can't participate in discussions in the room

Horse's Mouth

Ray DeFeis, an actor who has done this work: *"For me this work is about serving other artists. It's very gratifying when you feel that you've helped them improve in their field."*

Contact

Parsons tel. (212) 741-7576, F.I.T. tel. (212) 760-7650, or Institute of Design tel. (718) 855-3661.

Dialect Coach

Notes

Dialect Coach

Low Down
In this kind of work you help actors eliminate their regionalisms and accents (if they are getting in the way of their work) or teach them new dialects and accents for specific roles.

Scratch
$50-$150 an hour

Be
- Able to evaluate speech (a good ear)
- Able to imitate good and bad speech
- Observant
- Aware of the physical placement of speech and know how to teach a student to use it correctly
- Able to keep your students motivated during frustrating periods

Perks
- Seeing your students overcome their own regionalisms or apply a new dialect they've learned to their work is satisfying
- The money can be good
- The hours are flexible

Bummers
- Many young actors don't have the money to continue their lessons
- The work is irregular
- The work can be frustrating when a student isn't getting it

Horse's Mouth
Marci Meikle, a dialect coach: *"I feel that helping someone in this kind of work is a healing job. Helping people rid themselves of unwanted accents can free them to pursue their dreams."*

Contact
This is self-starter work. You must advertise in the trades and on bulletin boards wherever actors gather.

Club Date Singer
(called Occasionals in Los Angeles)

Notes

Club Date Singer
(called Occasionals in Los Angeles)

Low Down
Club date singers may sing either with one band or with many.
The work is at such occasions as weddings, Bar Mitzvahs, and
corporate conventions. The singer usually does a one hour set
with a ten minute break. You may do back-up work for another
singer as well as solo work.

Scratch
Varies: union scale is $183 for four hours work plus travel time
(Local 802, Musicians), but higher fees can be negotiated.

Be
- Comfortable on a stage in front of an audience
- Have a repertoire of songs and be comfortable with all styles of music
- Look good: have nice clothes, be well groomed
- Know your key for every song and know the necessary hand signals so you can "call your keys"
- Moving well on stage is a plus

Perks
- Sing songs that you love
- Meet all kinds of people
- Showcase your talents
- Go to great parties
- Travel

Bummers
- The pay is not great
- Late hours
- You need a nice wardrobe, so you run up cleaning expenses
- You have to provide your own means of transportation

Horse's Mouth
Norma Garbo, a club date singer: *"I'm an eclectic singer, I like all singing in all styles, and this work gives me that opportunity."*

Contact
You get most of this work word-of-mouth. Occasionally, you see
ads in trade papers for club date singers. Check out Local 802, the
musicians' union, for networking ideas.

Baton Teacher

Notes

Baton Teacher

Low Down

For some reason most baton teachers are women. In this kind of work you may teach in a classroom situation or privately. You work with students who'd like to learn baton twirling for parades and sporting events or just for the fun of it.

Scratch

$5 per student in a class, $25-$50 privately

Be
- An excellent twirler
- Able to demonstrate and explain all the moves
- Able to do the following moves: figure twirls, flat twirls, side twirls, ferris wheels, finger twirls, spins, and around the world
- Background in choreography is essential

Perks
- Seeing your students improve as they master the routines is gratifying
- If you enjoy baton twirling, you can get paid to do it

Bummers
- There isn't much of this work around
- In a classroom situation there isn't much money involved
- Some students are not capable of learning the routines, which can be frustrating

Horse's Mouth

Eileen Rosen, an actress and baton teacher: *"Ever since I was in high school I've loved baton twirling. The idea of making some extra money doing something I love is really a plus. Every time I see a girl master a routine it brings back some of the excitement I felt as a kid."*

Contact

The National Baton Twirling Association, P.O. Box 266, Janesville, Wisconsin 53547-0266. Check with some local schools to see if you can be contracted to teach as part of their curriculum.

Clown

Notes

Clown

Low Down
Everyone loves a clown! Clowns work at children's parties, corporate parties, and in circuses. You must genuinely love to make people laugh to do this kind of work.

Scratch
Varies: averages $175 a day, $25 an hour.

Be
- Willing to make a fool of yourself
- Love to entertain and make people laugh
- Be adept at magic, balloon animals and face painting for children's parties
- Agile
- Rehearse a patter that you can use with the magic tricks
- Comedic timing, dancing and singing are a plus

Perks
- The work is really fun
- Depending on the audience, stand-ups and singers may be able to try out new routines
- If you become successful, you can charge higher rates. especially at corporate parties

Bummers
- You can't do more than three or four hours of this a day: it's exhausting work
- Sometimes parents assume that part of your work is baby sitting
- Occasionally you have hecklers and drunks at corporate parties
- After a year of doing a lot of clown work, you usually need a break

Horse's Mouth
Herb Rothman, owner of the Clown Academy: "This kind of work can be truly rewarding, but there is much more to clown work than a prat fall. To really do well at parties, you must have a repertoire of tricks, bits, and comedy skills that'll keep even the most difficult audience entertained."

Contact
For clown training: New York Clown Academy (Herb Rothman); tel. (212) 777-6828; Ringling Brothers and Barnum and Bailey Clown Circus, Director of Admissions, 3201 New Mexico Avenue, NW, Washington, DC 20016. *For employment:* Best Clown (Willie Stewart); tel. (212) 777-6810. Try other party entertainment talent agents or advertise in magazines and on bulletin boards.

Television Game Show Contestant

Notes

Television Game Show Contestant

Low Down
Game show contestants can make huge amounts of money in a very short time. This is a very exciting way for actors to be seen and to make some good money to boot. Each show has its own rules for selecting contestants. To get on one, watch the show and learn how it's played. When you feel ready and think you have a shot at winning, contact the producers.

Scratch
Varies, from $0.00 to many thousands of dollars depending on which show you're on and how successful you are.

Be
- Enthusiastic
- Able to play the particular game well
- Outgoing, upbeat
- Knowledgeable of the categories covered by the game
- Enjoy competition
- Able to think quickly under pressure

Perks
- You can win a lot of money fast
- You get good exposure
- This work can be a lot of fun

Bummers
- Some game shows frown on actors playing (have to pay AFTRA fee, etc.)
- You could lose and/or not do well, which might be embarrassing

Horse's Mouth
Les McDonough, an actor who has been on game shows: *"Being on Password was my first television experience. It was really a lot of fun, but at times nerve wracking. The biggest problem with this kind of work is it's a dead-end kind of thing. You can't get on too many shows."*

Contact
At the end of each game show the producers are listed. Call them and ask what their requirements for contestants are
Here are a couple: Jeopardy: tel. (213) 466-3931; Wheel of Fortune (Merv Griffin Productions): tel. (213) 461-4701.

Sign Language Interpreter for Theater

Notes

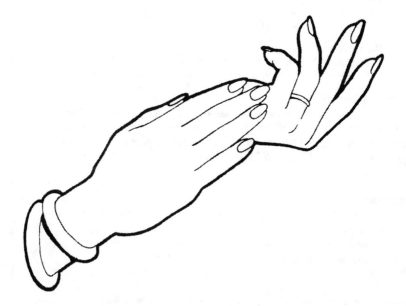

Sign Language Interpreter for Theater

Low Down

In this kind of work the interpreter uses sign language to interpret the play that is going on on stage. He usually gets the script well in advance, so he is familiar with it. Unless it's a one man show, there are usually a team of interpreters handling several roles each. In a production, interpreters have their own directors and deaf advisors. The goal of this work is to give the deaf audience as much of the performance as the hearing audience is getting.

Scratch

Up to $65-$70 an hour for a two hour minimum, depending on level of certification and work experience.

Be
- Fluent in the language. Sign language is not universal – it varies by country.
- Accomplished as an interpreter, with at least three years training in American Sign Language
- Able to turn speech into motion quickly
- Able to translate without getting in the way

Perks
- Some travel
- You meet fascinating people, as well as wonderful actors, and directors
- Helping others is satisfying
- You are part of wonderful productions

Bummers
- You have very little job security
- You don't have a pension
- You could develop Cumulative Trauma Disorder

Horse's Mouth

Katherine Diamond, a Broadway and television actor who is also a certified interpreter for the deaf: *"This type of work is not missionary work. Nobody is asking to be saved. I suggest before getting into this kind of work you ask yourself why you're doing it. I personally find this work very rewarding."*

Contact

To learn: Gallaudet University in Washington, D.C., (Liberal arts for the deaf); Union County College, Camden, New Jersey. *To work:* The local chapter of the National Registry for the Deaf (Maryland).

Social Dance Instructor

Notes

Social Dance Instructor

Low Down

Whenever most people think of social dance schools they think of the old Arthur Murray dance studios. These days, however, many professional dancers and actor/dancers are finding teaching social dancing a pleasant and in some cases very lucrative way to make extra money. Classes average 45 minutes to an hour. You may teach at an established school or start one yourself. Another way to teach dance is one-to-one coaching.

Scratch

Varies: $15-$250 a class, $25-$200 per hour.

Be
- A good dancer, able to demonstrate all the steps
- Outgoing and friendly
- Able to make dancing look easy and fun to do
- Able to find an enticing way to make even the most resistant newcomer interested in learning
- Up-to-date on the latest dances and steps
- Able to articulate to a dance student what is working and what is not working
- Patient

Perks
- It can be a fun job
- Seeing a once clumsy dancer really take off can be very satisfying
- If you start your own school or coach privately and are successful, you can make very good money.

Bummers
- No matter how hard you try or how good a teacher you are, there really are some people out there with two left feet
- It can be very difficult getting students at the beginning
- There are some initial expenses when you first set up your own business: studio rental, and advertising

Horse's Mouth

Blanche Hollerman, an actress who coaches social dancing:
"I can't begin to tell you what it feels like when you see 'Mister Clod', with the two left feet, actually move and dance gracefully. More often than not, this is a business of small miracles. It's usually the men who are the most resistant."

Contact

Dance Educators of America. To start your own studio, you must find a space, advertise in local papers, on bulletin boards, and put out the word that there's a dance studio in the neighborhood.

Theater Critic

Notes

Theater Critic

Low Down
For this book, we will only deal with reviewing plays as a part-time job with smaller newspapers like *Backstage* and local newspapers. When the major critics are busy, the smaller, less experienced critic is given the "stringer work." Theater reviewers are constantly trying to meet their deadlines. Their taste and opinions as well as how well they write determines how often they'll work.

Scratch
Varies widely: for small, local papers, can be $25 per review; for larger papers, full time, $12,500-$65,000.

Be
- Have good critical skills
- The more extensive your theatrical background the better
- Knowing theater history is helpful, especially for period plays

Perks
- Naturally all the shows you see are free
- You usually get the best seats in the theater
- If you love theater this is a wonderful job.

Bummers
- It's a highly competitive field. There are more critics than newspapers
- You work irregular hours
- Sometimes you must do hours of research before seeing a particular play

Horse's Mouth
Kevin Rheingold, an actor who has written for several small newspapers: *"For me the most difficult thing is seeing a really bad play being put on by a fledgling acting company. On the one hand you want to help keep them alive, but you're also responsible to your paper and readers. There are times I've shown up at a play and realized that I knew some of the actors who are performing personally. Even though I may feel conflicted, the bottom line is I must remain impartial."*

Contact
To get work on a specific newspaper, Leslie Hoban Blake, a critic for several newspapers, suggests that you send a query letter first and then follow it up with writing samples and clippings.

Dialogue Coach
(Television and Film)

Notes

Dialogue Coach
(Television and Film)

Low Down

Dialogue coaches are hired to help actors with their roles on a film or television show. Some are hired privately by the actor, some are hired by the producer, and some are hired by the director. Their job can range from helping the actor memorize lines to helping with script/character interpretation. Getting this kind of work is very political. You have to have the talent and know the right people.

Scratch

Varies widely, depending on what medium, and your experience. Average about $750 per week.

Be
- Trained in script interpretation and know the basics of how to rehearse actors properly
- Good with all kinds of people
- Have a solid background in acting and directing
- Able to work well under pressure
- Able to help actors find the important acting values within any script: Sit-com scripts and feature film scripts have different requirements

Perks
- You meet exciting people
- This can lead to future acting work
- With television, meeting the challenge of a new script each week is stimulating
- Seeing an actor grow into a role with your help is gratifying

Bummers
- On a sit-com there is a new set of rules every week
- The jobs are hard to find
- Sometimes the actors you work with aren't talented. You may be blamed for their lack of success
- Sometimes there is a bad chemistry between you and the actor you're working with.
- Actors with big egos can be a big pain in the neck

Horse's Mouth

Esther Rosen, an actress who occasionally does dialogue coaching: *"The thing I find most exciting is when I can find the right word that gets the correct response from an actor. You can get so frustrated running around in circles for hours until you say that one magic phrase that turns the light bulb on. It can be just a simple image like "imagine an ice cube going down your back."*

Square Dance Caller

Notes

Square Dance Caller

Low Down
The best way to learn to be a square dance caller is to apprentice at one of the over 7,000 clubs in the U.S. For the more earnest square dance callers there are also "callers colleges". Before you contact a college, you should have at least two years of square dancing experience.

Scratch
$60-$125 a night

Be
- Equipped with a good voice with clear diction
- Equipped with basic microphone skills
- Able to deal with large groups of dancers
- Possessed of a nice singing voice (doesn't have to be great)
- Knowlegeable of the many, many moves of this particular kind of dance
- In love with this kind of dancing, it shows in your voice

Perks
- It's a great, fun-filled job
- You get to make a lot of people happy
- It's a great way to meet people
- Callers get to travel all around the country

Bummers
- The requirements to be a caller are tough
- Occassional late hours
- If you're sick, you still have to show up and keep the energy in the room high
- If you work often, the travel can be exhausting

Horse's Mouth
Terry Rainer, an actor who used to do this kind of work: *"I'll tell you, when you get the room going, and everybody's having fun, there is no high in this world like what goes on in that room. And knowing that it all starts with you (and the band), it's a great feeling."*

Contact
To find out where all the clubs are, you should get a copy of the:
Square Dance Directory, P.O. Box 54055, Jackson. MS 39208
To find out where the colleges are: American Square Dancer, P.O. Box 488, Huron, OH 44839.

Radio City Rockette

Notes

Radio City Rockette

Low Down
The Radio City Rockettes are unquestionably the United States'
most famous dance troupe. The company is made up of 36
members (plus three replacements). According to Radio City, these
women are "ambassadors to the world. Part of their job is to
interact with all kinds of people wherever they go." Generally they
work 20 weeks during a year. During the Christmas holiday
season the Rockettes do up to 6 ninety minute shows a day.

Scratch
Varies: Radio City pays AGVA (American Guild of Variety Artists)
scale.

Be
• Between 18-30
• Between 5' 5-1/2" and 5' 8-1/2" in stocking feet
• Equipped with extensive tap, ballet, and jazz training
• In good physical condition, friendly and outgoing
• Long legs are a plus

Perks
• You are a part of this prestigious, world famous company
• You meet people all around the world
• Travel
• A feeling of family: Rockettes become very close
• The excitement of playing Radio City Music Hall, the Christmas show, and
  some great theaters internationally

Bummers
• The work can be grueling
• If you get hurt, especially with a leg injury, you're out of work

Horse's Mouth
The contact at Radio City: *"It really takes a special kind of person
to be a Rockette. We look for girls who are talented as well as
friendly and outgoing."*

Contact
Radio City Music Hall, 44 West 51st Street, New York, NY 10020
tel. (212) 247-4777. Note that all resumés are kept on file for two
years. If during that period they hold auditions, all girls on the list
will be notified no matter where they live.

Jingles Singer

Notes

Horse's Mouth

Norma Garbo, who has done this kind of work on occasion: *"To me
the greatest part about this work (aside from the money) is when
you click with great singers. I've gotten to sing with such singers as
Luther Vandroos and Patti Austen. Some of the greatest singers
make it into this kind of work."*

Contact

Because the money is so good in this field, it's a hard one to break
into. If you really think you have the talent, start by making demo
tapes and getting them out to agents, production houses, and
casting directors.

Jingles Singer

Low Down

For the select group who does most of this work, jungle singing is a very lucrative business. After spending less than an hour or two in a sound studio a jingle singer may make up to one hundred thousand dollars over a few years for a national thirty-second spot. Since the client may be spending $300-$350 an hour for studio time, the jingle singer is expected to arrive promptly, be able to pick up the jingle sheet music, learn it instantly, and hopefully get it exactly right on the first or second take. The client expects the singer to be able to "sell" the product with his or her voice. There are about 25 jingles singers who do about 80 percent of this work.

Scratch

Per session: SAG: solo, $333.30; 3-5 group, $187.95; 6-8 group $166.10; over 9, $133.00. AFTRA: solo, $185.00; 3-5 group, $136.40; 6-8 group $120.70; over 9, $107.15

Be
- Possessed of an excellent singing voice with excellent pitch
- Enthusiastic: it's important that the client and producers feel your excitment about their product
- Able to sight read music
- Able to sell a product instantly and believably with your voice
- Able to give the client what he wants on the spot, even if he doesn't know what it is
- SCHMOOZE factor: once you've proven you have the talent and can do the work, schmoozing with the client can be a real plus for future work

Perks
- The average session is often less than an hour
- You get to work with some incredibly talented people
- Connections in this field can lead to other singing work
- Because you're off camera, there is less fear of overexposure
- If you become part of the "in group" of jingles singers, you will work a lot and make a *lot* of money

Bummers
- The pressure to get it right and get it right soon is tremendous
- There is no audience. Some singers thrive on a live audience
- Very few make it in this field
- Before "making it" in this field there is a lot of work: demo tapes and auditions
- It is very cliquey: there's a definite "in crowd"

Cartoon Voices

Notes

Cartoon Voices

Low Down

In this kind of work, you must be able to synchronize your voice to animated characters on screen. According to Kent Harrison Hayes of Intersound, a Los Angeles sound studio, "You can expect it to take three days to do 22 minutes worth of work." Two of the biggies in this business were Mel Blanc (Bugs Bunny, Daffy Duck) and June Foray (Rocky, Bullwinkle). In some cases you synchronize your voice to the character on the screen, other times they "animate" your voice. Sometimes a character may just make "sounds." Each performer can do up to four character voices in a cartoon.

Scratch

Varies, depending on the length of the cartoon. Generally, $504 per day.

Be
- Versatile with your voice: You may be required to do up to four totally different voices in one cartoon. Multiple voices mean more work
- Able to make quick, definite choices: sometimes you are given the script right before you work
- Able to maintain the character voice throughout the whole cartoon

Perks
- The work is fun
- If you're good, this work is lucrative
- You don't have to memorize: you usually get the material after you arrive at the studio

Bummers
- Even if you are ill that day, you must work
- There is hardly any rehearsal time
- Your character voices cannot "blend". They must be totally different

Horse's Mouth

David Zema, an actor who specializes in voice-over work: *"I genuinely enjoy this kind of work. It can be fun and challenging at the same time. You learn to trust your instincts and make quick, definite decisions."*

Contact

Most of this work is in the Los Angeles area. Some possible leads: Hanna Barbera Cartoons: tel. (213) 851-5000 or Walt Disney (Burbank): tel. (818) 560-1000.

Foreign Film Dubbing Artist

Notes

Foreign Film Dubbing Artist

Low Down

In this kind of work, you either dub from another language into English or from English into another language. Kent Harrison Hayes, who works at Intersound in Los Angeles, says, "Generally, you dub an average of 10 to 15 lines per hour. It may take up to two or three weeks to do an entire film. This kind of work requires that actors know how to 'see-synch', that is, synchronize their voice to the voice on the film."

Scratch

Varies: the SAG session fee is $504 per day

Be

- Equipped with a good sense of rhythm
- Clever and think quickly on your feet
- Able to "see-synch"
- This work requires not only lip synching, but also good acting skills.
- You don't need to speak the language that you're dubbing, but you should be able to feel the correct word placements

Perks

- This work can be challenging and creative
- There is an increasing amount of this work coming in
- The work can be lucrative

Bummer

- The work can be tedious

Horse's Mouth

Kent Harrison Hayes, who has worked for nearly 15 years at Intersound Studios, a studio that does a lot of foreign film dubbing: *"The most important thing, I think, is that we're looking for good actors. For many years foreign film dubbing has been an under dog in the business. I believe it's finally coming into it's own these days, and we'd like to find the best talent to go with it."*

Contact

There are many sound studios both in New York and Los Angeles that do foreign film dubbing. Contact them directly, and then send voice tapes when requested.

Stunt Performer

Notes

Contact
There are many stunt associations in New York, including:

- East Coast Stuntmen's Assoc.
  P.O. Box 20712
  New York, NY 10025

- League of Independent Stunt Players
  P.O. Box 196
  Madison Square Station
  New York, NY 10159

- Stunt Specialists
  RD #2 Big Island Road
  Warwick, NY 10990

- Stunts, Inc.
  c/o Frank Ferrara
  Brooklyn, NY 11228

Stunt Performer

Low Down
If you're athletic, enjoy the adrenalin rush of danger, and thirst for thrills, this may be the work for you. Part of the excitement is realizing that many thousands of dollars may be at stake with just one take. This work includes car crashes, jumping off buildings, fights, and falling down stairs. The stunt coordinator creates the stunt, hires the stunt performers, and negotiates the fees, depending on the amount of danger involved.

Scratch
Varies widely, depending on the danger of the stunt. Utility stunt workers (somewhere between an extra and a stunt performer) start off at $504 per day.

Be
- Athletic and in good shape
- Able to get off on danger
- Physically coordinated
- Able to pay attention to minute details under pressure
- Timing is a life saving skill in this type of work

Perks
- You experience the thrill of doing the stunts
- A dangerous stunt can pay a lot of money
- There is a camaraderie among stunt actors
- Stunt jobs can lead to other acting work

Bummers
- You can get killed
- An injury can put you out of work for a long time
- You have to work your way up to get the better paying jobs, which involves both talent and politics
- Often you work in extremes of temperature
- For safety reasons, you may be stuck in very uncomfortable wardrobe for long stretches of time

Horse's Mouth
Bill Humphries, an actor who does stunt work: *"Stunt work has helped get me major exposure on feature films and television. It's hard to describe the adrenalin rush you get when doing a stunt and the satisfaction you feel after you've accomplished it."*

Monologue Coach

Notes

Monologue Coach

Low Down
Monologue coaches help actors identify the correct material for upcoming auditions. The psychological blocks an actor may be feeling about an audition must be dealt with. This job requires a vast knowledge of dramatic literature.

Scratch
Varies, averaging $45 an hour

Be
- PATIENT!
- Able to explain to actors where the problems are in their work
- Able to put actors at ease
- Well-trained and experienced in acting techniques

Perks
- The money can be good
- The schedule is flexible
- You are your own boss
- You get personal satisfaction when your student finally "gets it"
- You meet interesting people
- If you do a sufficient amount of this work, you can deduct home office expenses

Bummers
- Actors cancel at the last minute
- Students may lack motivation or become so frightened they don't return
- Working through actors' blocks can be frustrating and tiresome

Horse's Mouth
Jack Poggi, an actor who is also an audition coach: *"This work allows me to experiment freely and delve deeply into a monologue. It's a delight to see how quickly an actor can turn my suggestions into effect and do excellent work."*

Contact
This is self-starter work. If you really feel qualified to do this type of work, you should advertise in the trade papers, and on bulletin boards where actors meet.

Narrators

(Voice-Over Work for Industrial and Educational Films)

Notes

Narrators

(Voice-Over Work for Industrial and Educational Films)

Low Down

Remember when you were in school and saw those history or science movies and tried not to fall asleep? Well, the movies are usually more interesting and better made today. The voice you heard that told you about amoebas in the science movies or Thomas Jefferson in the history movies was the narrator. Basically, the narrator tells the story without appearing in the film. In industrial films, the narrator's voice must always sound like he knows exactly what he's talking about.

Scratch

Varies: generally, SAG rate is $504, AFTRA $311.50

Be
- Equipped with a well-trained voice that exudes confidence
- Get a copy of the N.B.C. Handbook of Good Pronunciation and learn correct pronunciation
- Practice reading for long stretches without stumbling over words
- Love reading
- Have a good command of the language

Perks
- You can work steadily in this field
- This work is lucrative
- If you like to read, this work will be enjoyable

Bummers
- The field is difficult to break into
- Material may be very technical or boring, and you must make it sound fresh and interesting

Horse's Mouth

David Zema, an actor who has narrated: *"I find this type of work very interesting and challenging. You must sound like you know, for instance, how to use a widget. You learn all kinds of things that normally you'd never have any reason to know about. The challenge is in acting like you've known all about widgets all your life."*

Contact

The best way to get this kind of work is by contacting producers and industrial agents who specifically do this type of work and sending them your voice-over reel.

Voice-Over Speaker
(for Television and Radio)

Notes

Voice-Over Speaker
(for Television and Radio)

Low Down

When you hear a voice on television, radio, or film and don't see the actor, that is a voice-over. Voice-over work is a growing field in show business. Everything from the voice on C.D. Roms for computers to a "tag" for a national television commercial is considered a voice-over, and the money can be BIG. Starting out in this business can be tough, since it is a very competitive market. Actors must make "demo" tapes with three or four samples of them doing commercial copy. The tapes should also include at least five character voices for work on cartoons and film, and they should not be any longer than three minutes.

Scratch

Varies: generally, SAG rate is $504 per session, AFTRA $311.50

Be
- Possessed of an extremely flexible voice
- Able to take very specific voice direction (*e.g.* "Make it smoother." "More bluesy." "Make it lighter.")
- There are voice-over schools in New York and Los Angeles where an actor can learn the technique

Perks
- Generally, voice-over sessions are very short: 15 minutes to an hour
- If you luck out and get a "tag" for a national television commercial, you can make a lot of money for very little work
- You can dress any way you wish for this work. No one cares how you look

Bummers
- Because no one sees your face, you miss out on on-camera exposure
- Voice-over sessions can be pressure-filled if the producer, director, and client are in conflict. Quite often, the talent is caught in the middle
- If you're sick the day of a voice-over session you must rise above it and give the client what he wants
- Very competitive

Horse's Mouth

David Zema, a successful voice-over actor and teacher: *"This is a great way to express yourself, have fun, and make some very good money for sometimes very little work. Generally voice-over people are entrepreneurs; they seek out and create their own jobs within the industry."*

Contact

Contact AFTRA, tel. (212) 532-0800, and SAG, tel. (212) 944-1030, to find out who accepts voice-over tapes.

PATH Actor

Notes

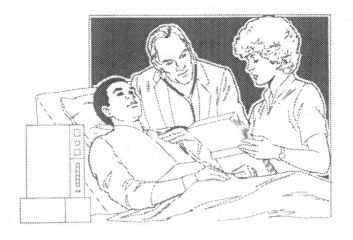

Professional Actors Training and Helping (PATH) Actor

Low Down
This actor-created group was formed three and a half years ago to help train doctors, medical students and interns. They have also worked on occasion with pharmaceutical companies. PATH-trained actors use improvisation to illustrate the needs of sick or dying patients. Their rehearsed scenarios give medical students an opportunity to learn the proper ways to interview a patient.

Scratch
Varies widely: from $150 for three hours work up to $1,000 a day.

Be
- Equipped with a strong background in improvisation
- A strong actor who can remain concentrated even in different playing environments
- Remember you are working with professionals and be able to act accordingly
- Able to think on your feet

Perks
- You get to hone your acting skills
- Helping others is very satisfying
- The money is very good
- Travel

Bummers
- This work can be emotionally draining
- The work can be irregular
- Each job has its own new set of circumstances. There are constant adjustments to be made

Horse's Mouth
Phil Levy, an actor and one of the creators of PATH: *"For me this work is incredibly rewarding. As an actor you get to work on some very challenging material. These people are dealing with life and death situations every day! Also it's a way to help teach the medical profession that the patient is an important part of the team. In reality so often the patient's input is neglected."*

Contact
Phil Levy at PATH; tel. (212) 229-2943.

Director and Choreographer for Live Industrials

Notes

Horse's Mouth

Margarie Beddow, an actress who has done this work: *"Working on these shows is great training. Sometimes you're pushed to your limits. It's a great way to expand your talent, widen your capabilities."*

Contact

Packagers for industrials often use agents who place directors. Occasionally, there are ads in the trades for directors, usually for a small show. The best way to get this kind of work is to work your way up, starting as an assistant to the director on one of the shows.

Director and Choreographer for Live Industrials

Low Down
Live industrials can be as big as a Broadway show or as compact as a small revue. They run the gamut from glitzy, overdone and garish to smart, stylized and tasteful. The purpose of a live industrial quite often is to show the company's salespeople and executives the new product line for the next year. The shows are very complex, quite often using films, slides and computer technology. There is a great deal of pre-planning that goes into a big industrial. Writers have to write the sketches, designers create sets and costumes and composers write original music dealing with the product of the company. The company has an image they want to project to their audience. The director/choreographer can be one person or two depending on the show's budget. For the purposes of this book, we will deal with the jobs of director and choreographer as part-time work. Indeed, since the end of the big money '80s, there are far fewer of these productions and most directors now only do this work part-time.

Scratch
Varies, depending on the size of the show, where it is and how long you work on it. Can be up to $10,000 or more for three weeks work.

Be
- Possessed of an extensive musical comedy directing background
- Able to work well under pressure
- Able to collaborate with all types, especially business people
- Able to handle a big musical audition
- A jack-of-all-trades
- Being a performer – acting, singing, dancing – is a plus

Perks
- You can make great money
- You meet all types of people
- You can be *very* creative
- You get to travel all over the world
- These jobs can lead to other work
- This is great training! You quickly learn what you can and can't do, creatively

Bummers
- You may have to work on a show whose book and music aren't the best, and you're required to make it shine
- The pressure can be tremendous
- The clients are powerful. Sometimes they interfere with your creative decisions
- Traveling with a show can be exhausting

Soap Opera Stand-In

Notes

Soap Opera Stand-In

Low Down

On some (not all) soap operas, stand-ins are used when the principle actor cannot be on the set (for dry rehearsal or occasionally for a run-through). The stand-in's job is to rehearse the scene with the other principle actors. Holding a script in hand, he rehearses the role of the actor he's standing in for. When the director gives notes to the actors during the rehearsal, it's the stand-in's job to carefully take the notes that are given to his actor. Later, the stand-in meets with the actor he's standing in for and gives him the director's notes.

Scratch

$19 an hour for a two hour minimum.

Be
- A well-trained actor
- Willing to take diligent notes
- Friendly and professional

Perks
- It's a good way to meet directors, stage managers, and other actors on a set
- It's a way to have your work seen
- It's quick work, usually over in a couple of hours
- If you do a good job, you'll be called constantly
- It's a way to watch working actors rehearse on the show and learn their techniques
- Since you're through so early, you have the whole day for auditions, classes, and other work

Bummers
- Usually you have to be there very early for dry run-through
- Being a stand-in is frustrating if it's for a role you feel capable of doing
- Sometimes you're given the script at the last minute and have to read it cold at the rehearsal

Horse's Mouth

Barbara Stein, an actress who does stand-in work: *"I find doing this work very enjoyable. It's easy, interesting, and since it's over so early, I have a whole day to do whatever I want in the city."*

Contact

Not all soaps use stand-ins. The best way to find out which shows do is to check with the extra/under five casting directors and let them know that you're interested.

Drama Coach

Notes

Contact

Starting out in this kind of work requires renting studio space, placing ads in the trades and signs on bulletin boards, producing pamphlets and mailings if you can afford it, and just getting out the word that you're available and good.

Drama Coach

Low Down
The job of the drama coach is to work with actors on specific material chosen either by the actor or by the coach. You may work on material for auditions or on style, acting problems, or specific blocks. The work can be done one-on-one or in a classroom situation. Monologues or scenes are either rehearsed at home or "cold-read" at the session. The drama coach critiques the work, offering suggestions and showing specifically where the problems are.

Scratch
Varies: $35-$200 an hour

Be
- Able to state specifically where a problem is occurring in an actor's work
- A skilled director
- Expert in different acting techniques, as well as having some training in speech, and movement
- Supportive (and not destructive)
- A person that acting students want to work with
- Acting experience is a big plus, but not always necessary

Perks
- The money can be very good, especially for private coaching
- Seeing an actor progress is rewarding
- This work can lead to private coaching on movie sets and television (See DIALOGUE COACH)
- Make your own schedule
- Can lead to future acting work for the drama coach

Bummers
- The work can be frustrating: students may be unable to break through emotional blocks, or not show up
- You may get an acting job and have to postpone the class
- Getting started in this kind of work can be difficult; it's a competitive field. Also, there is an initial investment for ads in trade papers, and space rental

Horse's Mouth
Catherine Wolf, a Broadway, television, and film actress who is also a drama coach: *"There is nothing as rewarding as helping students discover their own gifts. When you see your students open up and take risks in their work it's a very gratifying feeling."*

Drama Counselor

Notes

Contact
There are hundreds of overnight camps that hire drama
counselors. Check with agencies that hire summer help. Look for
ads in the New York Times, and other periodicals. Betsy Roper at
Camp Omni is always looking for good drama counselors. Tel.
(800) 386-6664.

Drama Counselor

Low Down
Being a drama counselor is seasonal work (summer). If you enjoy working with children and are able to direct big musicals on a very small scale, this may be the job for you. Summer camps all around the country hire drama counselors to direct anywhere from two to five shows a summer. Aside from the musical, the drama counselor may be required to write or find a short show for little children, run the talent show, and generally do any work that requires entertainment.

Scratch
Varies, averaging about $2,000 a summer.

Be
- Experienced, with a background in acting and directing
- Someone who LOVES working with kids
- PATIENT
- Energetic and supportive

Perks
- You get to spend an entire summer in the country
- You're not under the pressure of drama critics
- Being with children is rejuvenating

Bummers
- You can't be demanding, expecting the children to give up too much of their summer just to do your shows. It is a vacation camp, remember
- Trying to do a show in sometimes primitive circumstances can be frustrating
- Kids who can't memorize lines, and/or blocking are frustrating
- Generally, drama counselors have to live in the bunks with the kids. This can bring up a whole slew of problems, from lack of privacy to living in a pig sty

Horse's Mouth
Betsy Roper, owner of Camp Omni in Poland Springs, Maine:
"Drama counselors must be made aware that first and foremost this is a vacation for the kids. Although we'd love a wonderful production, it's the kids' fun that is most important. You can't coerce these kids into doing a show if they don't want to, nor can you make them spend every waking hour memorizing their lines."

Phone Program (Audio Tex) Recorder

Notes

Horse's Mouth

Gail Lubell, a voice-over actress who's done this work: *"For me it's the best work in the world. I've done jobs in 20 minutes and made $175 dollars. I've been lucky not having any problems with clients. I only accept jobs that are professional and in good taste. One job often leads to another."*

Contact

This kind of work you almost have to sniff out. Once you get involved with voice-over people, you'll hear about different jobs coming up. If you do well in this field, clients will recommend you to other clients and so on. This is a growing field.

Phone Program (Audio Tex) Recorder

Low Down

Audio tex covers a wide range of voice work for actors, from jobs as small as a professional tape for the local deli to 900 telephone number prerecorded tapes. The point of these tapes is to keep the caller interested even though they're dealing with a machine. I'll include a couple:

1.) PHONE PROGRAMS (AUTOMATIC ATTENDANT): When you call this number, you'll hear a prerecorded tape offering you services and information. You'll be told "Press 1 and you'll get such and such information". These tapes are often used on 900 numbers.

2.) NOVELTY TAPES: Entertainment tapes, such as those crazy voices for phone machines.

Scratch

Varies: negotiated by the actor. This is mostly non-union work. The average wage is $200 for up to two hours work.

Be

- Skilled at voice overs
- Have a flexible, adaptable voice
- Have a voice that can be commanding as well as friendly

Perks

- Quick and easy money
- Character voice work is fun
- Connections can lead to other work in the voice-over field
- Since you're not on camera, you can dress casually
- There is a lot of work for women in this field
- Since it's mostly non-union, you are your own boss
- If you're ambitious, you can drum up a lot of these little jobs

Bummers

- No union benefits
- Some of this work is sleazy: e.g. erotic phone tapes
- Sometimes you have to deal with unprofessional clients and work in an inadequate sound studio
- Since you don't have the union behind you on many of these jobs, you must fend for yourself if there's trouble

Audition Coach

Notes

Contact
This is another one of the "self-start" type jobs. Once you feel you are ready and prepared to deal with all the demands of the job, place ads in the trade papers, signs on bulletin boards where actors congregate and flyers. If you're good, people will find out and you're sure to have a blossoming business.

Audition Coach

Low Down
In this type of work, the audition coach prepares an actor for a specific audition. The actor sometimes brings the audition material (the sides) to the coach, and the coach and actor work together on the material. Their work includes interpreting the material as well as finding the best way for the actor to give a strong audition. The coach helps the actor find the most honest, solid choices. At other times the coach helps an actor find monologues and prepare for future auditions.

Scratch
Varies; negotiated. Usually about $50-$150.

Be
- Equipped with a solid acting and directing background, including background in theater history
- Have an encyclopedic knowledge of contemporary and classical monologues
- Know how to prepare the actor for the proper "mind-set" of an audition
- Able to instill confidence in an actor
- Able to immediately assess an actor's strengths and weaknesses and make them work for him or her at the audition
- Classical training and style are a must!

Perks
- The hours are flexible
- Experiencing the joy of seeing an actor finally "get it"
- The money can be good
- Meeting wonderful actors who may eventually become major stars

Bummers
- The field is over-crowded
- The costs of studio rentals and publicity are constantly going up
- Competition with talent agents, casting directors, and others who are not qualified to be audition coaches yet dangle the carrot of work before unsuspecting young actors

Horse's Mouth
Bob Dagny, an acting coach in New York: *"When you find the center of a committed actor's individual talents and are able to channel it along with his personality into a strong audition, it's a wonderful feeling of accomplishment for both of you."*

Industrial Film Actor

Notes

Horse's Mouth

Linda Gallant, an actress who has done industrials: "I've learned a great deal about how to work on camera by doing industrials. It's given me a comfortable income and I've learned a lot about many different businesses. I find the work interesting and always challenging."

Contact

More and more talent agents are now handling industrial films. Check with SAG as to which agents and production houses now handle this type of work.

Industrial Film Actor

Low Down
The SAG handbook describes Category I industrials as "programs designed to train, inform, promote a product, or perform a public-relations function, and are exhibited in classrooms, museums, libraries, or other places where no admission is charged". School educational films on various subjects are one example, business films for employees which discuss new products would be another. Category II industrials, according to SAG, are "intended for unrestricted exhibition to the general public." They're shown at "public places such as coliseums, railroads stations, air terminals, or shopping centers." A group of actors and spokesmen are usually hired to work in what is usually an episodic or storytelling format. Actors who are specific types and character men and women find this field most lucrative, as do spokespeople.

Scratch
The SAG-covered industrials are broken down into two categories: I) In house: $364; II) General public: $452. There are also many non-union industrials whose fees are negotiated.

Be
- Able to play the various types in the business world, from blue collar to CEO, convincingly
- Have a confident voice and attitude on camera
- Able to make some very technical mumbo-jumbo sound everyday
- Provide your own wardrobe: you're paid $15 for each change that you bring

Perks
- Blacks, Hispanics, and other minorities are given better opportunities in these films than in commercial films
- You don't have to be a beauty or even exceptional-looking to work on these films
- It's a safe place to get on-camera experience and get paid for it
- There is a lot of work
- One job quite often leads to many more in this field
- Travel: many of these shoot out of town

Bummers
- The material can be very technical and boring
- Sometimes they don't have a teleprompter, and you must therefore memorize a great deal of difficult material
- The working conditions can be amateurish
- The material may be so technical that showing it outside this field won't serve you in any way.

Film Extra

Notes

Horse's Mouth

Regine Allen, an actress who has recently started doing extra work: *"I've just arrived in New York, and for me being on a set, working with pros, getting my feet wet, it's all a great learning experience."*

Contact

Contact the casting directors. In Los Angeles, Central Casting; in New York try Sylvia Fay Casting 71 Park Ave, New York, NY 10010, Wilfley Todd Casting, 60 Madison Ave, Room 1017, New York, NY 10010, tel. (212) 685-3537, Amerfilm, 375 Broadway 3R, New York, NY 10017, tel. (212) 334-3882, and others.

Film Extra

Low Down

Film extras are seen and not heard. They are the actors walking behind or past the principle player. They are one of the elements that give a scene in a movie a realistic sense. In some scenes, film extras are expected to react to a situation (*i.e.* a crowd running away from the monster in horror!); in others, they surround the principles and add "atmosphere" (*i.e.* romantic couples dancing around our stars who have finally fallen in love). Some extra calls involve only a few extras, others hundreds. Extras are "typed" by extras casting directors (*i.e.* upscale, blue collar). Some calls require n.d. (nondescript) extras for their background. Extras should have wardrobe that is appropriate to their type (for all seasons). According to Central Casting in Los Angeles, who cast extras, extras should always show up "camera ready" (dressed up, made up, and ready to work).

Scratch

In New York rates start at $99 and goes up with penalties, and overtime. The rates are different in Los Angeles.

Be

- Available. Extra work is one of the "hurry up and wait" jobs. You are expected to be ready to go to set on a moment's notice, even though that moment may take hours
- Have patience: it can be a long day
- Know how to realistically mime a conversation without speaking, especially if you're near a boom microphone, or near the principles
- Listen attentively to all directions: they may change in the next take
- As in all film acting, your gestures and actions should be small

Perks

- With enough of this work, you qualify for free health insurance and a pension
- You can be upgraded to a principle role
- You gain on-camera experience
- This work gives you an opportunity to network with other actors
- You see great film directors and actors work

Bummers

- The days are sometimes LONG
- Extras "holding areas" can be dirty and cluttered
- Extras are not always treated with great respect
- You may have to work in extremes of weather
- Sometimes you're out of the city, can't get to a phone, and miss getting important messages for work

Body Double or Photo Double

Notes

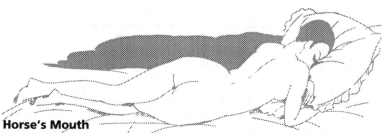

Horse's Mouth

Jim Green, at Central Casting in Los Angeles: *"This kind of work is very specific. There aren't that many calls for it, and generally a few actors get all the work."*

Contact

Central Casting in Los Angeles or other agencies that handle body doubles. Many "extras casting" people cast photo doubles; check in with them.

Body Double or Photo Double

Low Down

Remember that hot, steamy love scene with your favorite movie star in her last movie? Did you notice how beautiful her body was? Guess what? In many cases that wasn't the star's body but her body double's. Body doubles replace the star in certain scenes because the star is modest or may not have the best body. Body doubles, however, usually have more idealized, almost perfect, bodies. "In movies we strive to create fantasy," says one body parts casting director. There are body double actors who do this work almost exclusively.

A photo double is an actor who looks like a specific star. The photo double will be photographed in "long shots": from behind, walking away from camera, and in other shots that don't require the acting talents of the star.

Scratch

Body double is negotiable: for nudes, starts at about $500 a day. Photo double: $75 in L.A., more in New York.

Be
- In great shape, have an excellent body
- Able to "match" the position the star was just in and continue the action (*i.e.* lovemaking), keeping the continuity
- Have little or no modesty and feel totally confident with your body on camera
- Photo double actors should be able to walk like the actor they're replacing

Perks
- Body doubling can be very good money
- Although you may be in compromising positions, since you're replacing the star, the camera never sees your face
- If you click with specific stars, you may end up doing their body double and photo double work in other films
- These jobs may lead to other work in the business

Bummers
- This work can be frustrating. Since your face is never seen, you are not really identifiable
- Your body must always be in tip-top shape: rigorous dieting and exercise
- Photo doubling is sometimes a dead-end street

Theatre-Dance Video Performer

Notes

Theatre-Dance Video Performer

Low Down

Arising out of the performance art field, these multi-media pieces use actors, dancers, and many technicians. Each piece has its own style, concept, and form. Theater dance video work uses actors and dancers both live and on video. Because this is still a burgeoning field, it is hard to say how much work actors will find here, but, as one director said, "The future looks very exciting for all performers in this type of work."

Scratch

Varies widely: this is a new field, so all wages are negotiable.

Be
- Skilled, with a strong background in dance and/or theater
- Comfortable working with video technology
- Adaptable to the vision of the work
- Have ensemble experience

Perks
- This is a very creative field, full of possibilities
- You get to work with very creative people
- You have an opportunity to promote yourself and showcase your work
- In much of this work, everyone in the ensemble is given a "star turn"
- You get the opportunity to do ensemble work

Bummers
- The money in this field is not great yet
- There are rehearsal frustrations in working in new concepts or forms
- Being adaptable and working with the technology can be difficult and even dangerous

Horse's Mouth

Ariane Smith, an innovator in this field who is presently working on a piece: *"All the people I'm involved with in this kind of work are doing it not only for the art but also for the issues involved. Much of this work is political in nature. But bottom line, it's just damn fun to do!"*

Contact

There are constantly ads in the trades and in downtown papers for this kind of work. Ariane Smith can be reached at (212) 242-0955.

Novelty Performer

Notes

Contact

The best way to start out in this field is to contact specialty, novelty talent agents. At the beginning, it may be rough, but once you get into the circuit you can quickly build up a reputation and a clientele of repeat customers.

Novelty Performer

Low Down

This is theme party work at corporate parties, children's parties, holiday parties, or special occasions. Actors dress up in all kinds of costumes and characters, depending on the party theme, and interact with the party guests. The goal is simple: entertain the guests! Generally, you work for forty minutes and take twenty off. You make balloon animals, paint faces, do magic tricks, sing, dance, whatever.

Scratch

Varies widely, averaging $50-$150 an hour, including travel time.

Be
- An excellent performer
- Uninhibited
- Sensitive to individual people's moods
- Able to gauge the party
- A people person
- Quick on your feet. An improv background is helpful
- This work is about having fun and helping others to have fun

Perks
- The work is fun
- Meet interesting people
- The money is good
- Go to great parties, have great food
- Try out new songs, and materials
- Work when you want to work

Bummers
- Sometimes there are drunks to deal with
- Guests sometimes hit on you
- Sometimes, no matter how hard you try, the chemistry at the party just doesn't work
- Not knowing what you're walking into with each gig can be scary
- Sometimes you have to travel to out-of-the-way places
- This work has been drying up a bit over the last few years

Horse's Mouth

Ariane Smith, who does this kind of work: *"Basically, you work magic for people. It's your job to help break the ice, make the party happen. It can be great fun!"*

Live Industrial Actor

Notes

Contact

Check for ads in the trades. Try agents who handle industrials. If you ask around where singers and dancers are hanging out, you'll be able to find out where the next auditions are.

Live Industrial Actor

Low Down

Live industrials offer actors, singers and dancers all sorts of entertainment work. Some of these shows are well-budgeted with fancy costumes, extravagant sets, lights, and technology. Some of the most creative people in show business lend their talents (for a pretty penny) to making these information-based productions really fly.

The purposes of industrials are many: to inform salespeople of a new line, to motivate a company's employees, reward top employees, entice corporate investors, etc. Actors are called upon to do things as silly as "sing the praises of a new spark plug". Some of it may seem ridiculous, but there's a lot of money floating around in this field. Actors shouldn't turn their noses up so fast.

Scratch

Varies. Equity minimum is $804 a week and up. For seven days to two weeks, $1,006. For work less than a week: $287 for the first day, $144 for each day thereafter.

Be
- Able to sing, dance, and act
- Friendly, outgoing
- A quick study: sometimes re-writes happen fast
- Having a novelty act is a plus in this field: it may be worked into the show

Perks
- The money is very good
- Travel: some shows go all over the world
- Work with some of the top creative people

Bummers
- Making seemingly silly material significant, important, and entertaining can be difficult
- Rehearsals can be exhausting
- Last minute re-writes and changes are common

Horse's Mouth

Ingrid Zaslow, an actress/dancer who has done this work: *"I know it can be silly, but it can also be a lot of fun. It's a great way to meet and work with some of the best people in the business. Industrials have opened many doors for me and lead to a lot of other work."*

Music Video Performer

Notes

Music Video Performer

Low Down
Actors, singers, and dancers are all hired for these "mini-musicals" made to promote a performer's latest song. The call can be for model types as well as off-beat street types. Music videos are all about "the look". For dancers, there are dance auditions, and actors may have to audition for short acting vignettes in the video.

Scratch
Varies widely. Although there are some SAG music videos, most of these fall between the cracks. An average salary is $200 to $500 per video, but they can go as low as $75.

Be
- Able to dance and/or act
- Have a background of on-camera work
- Have endurance and stamina: sometimes these shoot for long hours

Perks
- These jobs can be good exposure
- You may work with some top directors and top stars
- The work is quick: usually a one shot deal
- A film director shooting the video may want you for feature work

Bummers
- The hours are long
- These jobs may pay very little money
- There are no residuals

Horse's Mouth
Caroline Sinclair, a casting agent who occasionally casts the music videos: *"This kind of work can be good on-camera training and can be a way of making contacts for other work in show business."*

Contact
There are several casting directors, including Caroline Sinclair, who cast videos from time to time. There are constantly ads in the trades for this kind of work.

Non-Broadcast Video Actor

Notes

Horse's Mouth

Kathy Luster, an actress who does this work: *"I find this work very creative. Although it may be difficult at times doing this work, when you get through it and see the finished product it's very rewarding."*

Contact

Most agents don't handle this work (yet). One way to find out who's doing what in this field is to check out different technical trade papers. You'll see ads looking for technical crew members for non-broadcast videos. Another way is good old word-of-mouth. Once you break into this field, you'll see there are a lot of jobs available, and you can work steadily.

Non-Broadcast Video Actor

Low Down

Non-broadcast videos include training videos, how-to videos, and instruction and information videos. The latest trend in this fast-growing field is in interactive video and C.D. Rom. Actors are finding all sorts of work here, from spokesman to character work. Actors who have a television commercial background seem to find this an especially good field.

Scratch

Varies widely. This work is mainly non-union, so the fees are negotiated. Pay can range from $100 to $1,000 per video.

Be
- Able to use a teleprompter or have and know how to use an ear prompter
- Able to work well on your feet
- Able to portray recognizable types
- On-camera training and experience are helpful
- Pleasant, have a commanding voice and good voice-over techniques

Perks
- There is a lot of work in this field
- You get invaluable on-camera experience
- Unlike with commercials, there is no fear here of overexposure
- The tapes can be used to show a sampling of your work
- Actors are often allowed to offer their input during shooting
- This work can be very creative
- You don't have to memorize a lot of lines

Bummers
- There are no residuals
- This work is difficult to break into
- There are very few union jobs
- The hours can be long
- You must buy your own ear prompter, which can cost up to $1,000
- Quite often, you must do your own hair and make-up
- You must provide your own wardrobe
- On the set or at a location you may have few amenities
- You don't know from job to job what the set will be

Production Assistant (P.A.) on a Movie

Notes

Contact

Finding much of this work is word-of-mouth. Check Local 771's (film editors' union) lists to see what's coming up, then send resumés. Check the *Village Voice* for leads.

Production Assistant (P.A.) on a Movie

Low Down

This is considered entry-level work for getting into movies. Occasionally, actors will do it just to see what it's like working at the production level. The job includes on-location traffic management, dealing with extras, herding extras into holding areas, dealing with extras vouchers, just about anything that needs to be done. To move up in movies you need three sponsors; being a P.A. is one way of getting them.

Scratch

Varies, averaging $100-$175 a day.

Be
- Have a film background or training at a film school
- Have endurance: the days can be very long
- Patient: things can go very slowly on a movie set
- Able to put up with all types of temperaments
- Able to deal with pressure-filled situations

Perks
- This can be a way to move up in movies
- You get to meet movie stars
- You learn by doing on a movie set
- You can make contacts for other work

Bummers
- Very long hours
- Weather can be treacherous
- You are considered the bottom of the totem pole
- You have to deal with crazies on the streets

Horse's Mouth

John Farkas, who has worked on several movies as a production assistant: *"Even though it can be tough work, it can definitely be fun. There is an aura that's very exciting about being on a movie set, especially big budget, big star movies. You always know you'll meet interesting people and get to see how some top directors work."*

Soap Opera Extra

Notes

Contact

Each soap opera has an extra, under five casting director. Get a copy of the Ross Reports, which lists who they are and how to contact them. The Ross Reports, tel. (718) 937-3990, can be purchased at most drama bookstores.

Soap Opera Extra

Low Down
Soap opera extras usually work in a television studio. Actors are typed and assigned different scenes to work. The soap opera extra creates the atmosphere of a scene.

Scratch
AFTRA rate is $128 per day.

Be
- Comfortable working on a television set
- Have an acting background
- Have a good wardrobe
- Able to take directions well
- Able to mime a conversation

Perks
- Since you're working in a studio, you're not affected by weather
- Generally, the calls are not too early: 9 or 10 A.M.
- This can be very pleasant work
- You get a chance to watch the contract players work
- Generally, the day is not too long
- Since you're assigned specific scenes, you generally know when you'll be working
- This is a good opportunity to network with other actors
- Can be upgraded to an under-5

Bummers
- Some casting people consider this work demeaning if you're a serious, ambitious actor
- On some sets, there is a subtle caste system in which the extras are low on the totem pole
- If 20 or more extras are hired, there is a twenty percent reduction in salary

Horse's Mouth
Kenny Adler, who has done extra work on soaps: *"I found the work very enjoyable for a while. If you're interested in doing principle work on soaps it's a great way to see how the actors work. When I started getting under five's and day players I was advised not to continue doing extra work and so I stopped."*

Stand-Up Comic

Notes

Contact

There is a professional comedians association. Contact Comedy U.S.A., 401 East 81st Street, New York, NY 10028. In L.A., Dramalogue, the trade paper, lists the comedy clubs. In New York, there are many comedy clubs. When you feel ready, contact them to find out when you can try it out

Stand-Up Comic

Low Down
Comics work alone, in pairs, or in comedy troupes. The job is always the same: to make people laugh. Comics work in comedy clubs, theaters, television, and movies. Every comic has to develop some persona, even if it's "just this guy telling some jokes." Comics try out new material all the time at different comedy clubs. Some comics tell stories; others tell jokes. Beginning comics usually get a shot on off nights at comedy clubs.

Scratch
Varies widely: from a percent of the door at comedy clubs to many thousands of dollars in Las Vegas, on television, and in movies.

Be
- FUNNY – HAVE A SENSE OF HUMOR!
- Able to deal with hecklers
- Comfortable in front of audiences
- Able to develop routines and write jokes
- Have comic timing
- Have an unusual slant on things

Perks
- These jobs can lead to television and motion picture work
- A successful stand-up comic can make a lot of money
- You get to enjoy making an audience laugh

Bummers
- You can have a bad night
- You have to deal with hecklers
- Sometimes you're up last and most of the audience is gone
- At the beginning the money is bad
- Developing an audience can be tough at the beginning
- Getting agents and talent scouts to see your work is difficult at the beginning

Horse's Mouth
Kenny Kramer, a former stand-up comic, whom the character "Kramer" on the Seinfield show was based on: *"If you're funny, there's an incredible amount of money and first class everything."*

Award Show Stand-In

Notes

Award Show Stand-In

Low Down
Award shows such as the Grammy's and the Tony's, use actors as stand-ins during the final tech rehearsals. Actors are selected to stand-in for the stars who will be attending the show.

Scratch
AFTRA rate is $19 an hour for a two hour minimum.

Be
- Able to read the teleprompter, dance, sing and ad lib
- Able to take direction and immediately do what's asked of you
- Able to work well under pressure
- Able to retain pertinent information
- Comfortable on a big stage with lots of technical work going on
- Singing and dancing are a plus

Perks
- It's very exciting work
- You meet a lot of celebrities
- If you do well, you're asked back year after year
- There's usually overtime, which is good money

Bummers
- The work can be exhausting
- Only a select group get this work every year
- Because of the pressure, you're not always treated kindly

Horse's Mouth
Barbara Stein, an actress who has done award show stand-in work: *"Working on award shows can be a wonderful experience. You learn how to take direction, work on your feet, use a teleprompter, and trust your instincts."*

Contact
The best way to find out about this work is word-of-mouth. Since many of the same people are used year to year it may be difficult to break into, but if you persevere you may be able to get in.

College Guest Director

Notes

College Guest Director

Low Down

A C.G.D. works at a college in the theater arts department and directs one show. This includes casting, pre-production work, rehearsals, and performance (generally 3-7 performances). The director is expected to teach one masters' class in theater and to live in residence at the college.

Scratch

Varies, depending on your credentials. Average $1,000-$5,000 and up.

Be
- Experienced, with directorial as well as teaching skills
- Patient since you are working with neophyte actors
- Able to make do with limited resources: in some colleges you may not have the best technical equipment

Perks
- This kind of work not only helps the students but also builds up your own creative reserves
- The money can be excellent
- Travel
- A college production is generally a safe learning experience: New York critics are not invited
- Seeing young actors' talents soar is rewarding

Bummers
- This work puts you out of commission as an actor.
- The technical staff may be untrained
- There are scholastic pressures on the students, so they are not always available when you need them

Horse's Mouth

Andre DeShields, an actor who has guest-directed at colleges:
"Simply put, if you want to become a better actor then direct young actors."

Contact

Much of this work comes about when a college directly contacts a specific actor. On occasion, there are ads in the trades. If you put out feelers through the grapevine, you may hear of a college looking for a guest director.

Exotic Dancer

Notes

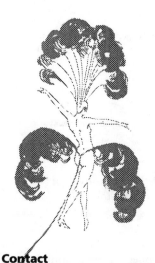

Contact
The best way to get this work is to go to the clubs and apply in
person. There are constantly ads in the trade papers and
newspapers.

Exotic Dancer

Low Down
By now I'm sure you've heard of the male dancers of Chippendales and you may have heard of Runway 69's lady dancers. Both of these clubs (as well as many others) hire actor/dancer/models to perform in sometimes elaborately choreographed shows where titillation is the main entertainment. The dancers, usually scantily clad, dance alone or in groups of up to seven or eight. Generally they dance for 30 minutes and are then off for up to 30 minutes. Most of these dancers are hired because of their physical beauty.

Scratch
Varies widely, depending on the club and the night. Average $200-$700 a night and up.

Be
- Attractive with an excellent body
- Have some dance experience
- Able to create some kind of an aura with the audience: e.g. seductive or mysterious
- Comfortable dancing for up to 30 minutes with hardly any clothes on: exhibitionists are welcome in this kind of work

Perks
- The money can be incredible
- If you enjoy exciting an audience, this may be the work for you
- There is a camaraderie between the dancers, a feeling of family

Bummers
- Most of these clubs are smoke-filled
- The hours are very late
- You may be harassed by customers
- Some people consider this sleazy work
- Some of the lesser clubs expect you to hustle drinks from customers
- Obsessive fans can be dangerous

Horse's Mouth
Ilyse Cameron, an actress who has been an exotic dancer: *"The money in this work can be so incredible that it's hard to break away. Ironically, some of the girls are in college, mothers, stuff like that. I only did it for a few months one summer, and let me tell you it can be a real ego builder. I know it's not considered the most up and up work, but I dealt with it as just another form of entertainment."*

Headshot Photographer

Notes

Headshot Photographer

Low Down
Headshot photographers photograph actors. This requires meeting with actors, showing them your portfolio of work, taking the photographs, reviewing their contact sheets with them, and helping them select the best head shots. Increasingly, actors are doing this work part-time. The idea is that an actor will know best what other actors need for their headshots.

Scratch
Varies widely: $150-$1,000 a week.

Be
- Know camera techniques
- Know lighting and have an eye for composition
- Have your own style, something that sets you apart from other photographers
- Know how to listen to actors to see what they're looking for in a headshot
- Have a good sales technique: be able to book the job
- Express a confidence and belief in your work
- Able to apply acting skills to a session

Perks
- You meet all kinds of people
- It's another creative outlet
- You make your own hours, are your own boss
- You feel a great deal of pride when you do a good job and the client is satisfied
- You can work at home
- This work has a very low start-up cost

Bummers
- Some actors will never be satisfied no matter how well you photograph them
- Actors may not show up
- Outdoor shoots are filled with problems
- Some actors are very tempermental and difficult to work with

Horse's Mouth
Danny Darrow, an actor who shoots actor headshots: *"This is a great way to make extra money. I find the work really creative and enjoy meeting all kinds of people. If I have to do something other than act for money I'm glad this is it."*

Contact
Pub an ad in the show business trades. Place pamphlets or cards with your name and phone number in places where actors meet. Have your friends spread the word.

Dance Therapist

Notes

Dance Therapist

Low Down
A dance therapist helps people with emotional problems find ways to express themselves through dance. Dance therapists working along with physical therapists, doctors, psychologists and nurses also help handicapped clients. There is no set way of working; each patient's needs determine the therapy.

Scratch
Varies widely: generally, about $20 an hour.

Be
- Have a Masters Degree in dance therapy
- Patient: progress can be very slow
- Understand thoroughly how the body works
- Feel comfortable working intimately with various kinds of people
- Know a variety of ways to demonstrate different movements

Perks
- Helping another human being is gratifying
- In freelance work, you can make your own schedule
- Breakthroughs are very satisfying

Bummers
- This work can be frustrating
- You can not allow yourself to have any emotional attachments to your clients
- You must undergo thorough training at substantial cost.

Horse's Mouth
Gerald Greer, an actor/dancer who is also a dance therapist: *"I have been doing more and more dance therapy work and less acting the last few years. The reason is I find dance therapy in many ways more rewarding. I may miss the audience applause after a performance, but seeing a client have a breakthrough (for me) is much more fulfilling."*

Contact
The American Dance Therapy Association.

Piano Bar Piano Player

Notes

Piano Bar Piano Player

Low Down
The piano bar player plays in small clubs. He's expected to have an extensive repertoire of songs. He should be able to gauge or control the enthusiasm and tone in the room. He should be able to accompany the audience if they want to sing. The best piano bar piano players always have a mellow smile and a pleasant repartee with the people in the room. Good piano bar piano players always keep smiling even though they've just sung "New York, New York", for the hundreth time.

Scratch
Vary widely: The average club pays $50-$75 plus tips for three-six hours work.

Be
- Have a pleasant singing voice and play piano in various styles well
- Know a lot of popular songs by heart
- Cordial, friendly, and pleasant
- Exude a calm confidence in your playing and singing abilities

Perks
- Sometimes the tips can be good
- A good piano bar piano player can usually find work
- You are free to work when you want
- These jobs are a nice way to meet people and get free drinks
- It's a great place to try out new material

Bummers
- Late hours
- Smoke-filled rooms
- Belligerent drunken customers
- No job security
- No benefits

Horse's Mouth
Gary Kahn, a singer/actor who's played piano bars: *"This work is for the performer who enjoys night life and a bar atmosphere. It's informal and a pleasant way to perform and earn some extra money."*

Contact
The best way to find this work is to go directly to the piano bar you want to work in. There are "off nights" you may be able to start on. Piano players come and go, so a good piano bar piano player can usually find work somewhere. There are also ads in the trades.

Modeling Teacher

Notes

Modeling Teacher

Low Down
Actors and models are hired by modeling schools to teach: confidence building techniques, speech, poise, television commercial technique, exercise, posture, etiquette, photo posing, wardrobe, make-up, hair, and acting. The actor/model is generally hired in three hour shifts and is expected to be well groomed, polite and supportive of the students. Most modeling schools have a training session where they teach their future teachers the curriculum.

Scratch
Varies: generally, about $15 an hour.

Be
- Have a "put together" look
- Refined and have poise
- Have a warm personality
- A supportive instructor

Perks
- You can book in or book out depending on your schedule
- It's a way of helping people
- The atmosphere is friendly

Bummers
- Classes can be overcrowded
- Some students are slow and need more help
- Sometimes you must prepare on your own time for a class

Horse's Mouth
Juanita Boyle, a former director of modeling at the Barbizon modeling school: *"The modeling teacher gives his students confidence and makes them aware of the possibility for a better future. When I was at Barbizon we always were looking for people in the performing arts. We found that performers were friendly, outgoing and articulate, all very important in this kind of work."*

Contact
The two biggest modeling schools are Barbizon, tel. (212) 239-1110, and Casablanca's. They have franchises all over the country. Occasionally, the trades will have ads looking for modeling teachers.

Back-Up Singer

Notes

Back-Up Singer

Low Down
A back-up singer's job is to make the lead singer look and sound good. He or she must harmonize and blend well and be comfortable as a "supporting" stage performer. Singers with too distinct a voice don't do well in this kind of work. It's really the perfect job for the singer who loves to sing on stage but doesn't want the pressure of being a star.

Scratch
Varies widely, depending on your experience, who you're doing back-up for, and what kind of club you're in: average $50-$150 a night.

Be
- Well groomed with stage presence and a voice that's able to harmonize well
- Able to sight read and learn music quickly
- Able to improvise your part vocally: it may not be on the sheet music
- Vocal versatility is a big plus

Perks
- Great experience for beginning singers
- A wonderful opportunity to network
- Travel
- Some singers move up with big name stars and sing on their recordings

Bummers
- You have no say about the choice of material
- You may have to wear a costume that you don't like
- Some stars are "divas", with temperaments
- You may have to rehearse a lot for little money

Horse's Mouth
Gary Kahn, an actor/singer who has done back-up work: *"Doing back-up, aside from a way to make a buck, is a good way for beginning singers to get their feet wet and see what's out there."*

Contact
At the beginning, the best way to get this work is word-of-mouth. There are constantly ads for back-up singers in the trades and on bulletin boards where performers hang out.

Actor-Video Creator and Director

Notes

Actor-Video Creator and Director

Low Down

More actors are getting into this field. Actors think that they're exceptionally qualified to help other actors create an audition/sample video. The actor/clients brings in a tape that shows range, type, and skills. The director chooses the material that he feels will show them off best. Sometimes actors want the director and crew to come to the theater where they're performing and shoot a scene from the show. Another common request is for the director to shoot the actor in a mock interview set up.

Scratch

Varies: averages $100 an hour before paying studio time and camera operator.

Be
- Able to use all the necessary equipment
- Have access to a good working space
- Know lighting and composition
- Sensitive to actors' needs
- Able to calm nervous actors so that they can do their work

Perks
- The money is good
- You enhance actors careers
- You meet people, make contacts

Bummers
- Each job has unique problems and anxieties
- Actors are often difficult to work with
- Time is money in a studio, and actors don't want to pay for extra time even though they might need it

Horse's Mouth

Johnathan Perry, a director at Video Portfolios: *"Quite often actors don't have a clear concept of what they want. Part of the challenge of this work is helping them find what they're looking for and shooting it as they see it."*

Fit Model

Notes

Fit Model

Low Down

The job of a fit model is to try on garment after garment for a manufacturer. The fit model's perceptions about how the garment feels, fits, and sometimes looks are very important to the company. The model must have specific proportions to do this work (be an exact size). Her feedback is an important element in this work. The model may work from two to five times a week for one or two hour sessions.

Scratch

Varies: agencies generally charge $150 (plus 25%) an hour for this work. Without an agency, the fees are negotiated.

Be
- Fashionable and stylish
- Articulate, able to describe fit specifically
- Your measurements are a major factor in getting this work

Perks
- Flexible schedule
- Good money
- Models get to keep some of the clothes
- Models are given vacation time with pay

Bummers
- The work can be very demanding
- You're under constant pressure
- Models must maintain their exact size

Horse's Mouth

Carrie Arlins, an actress who does fit modeling: *"I've always loved fashion and clothes, so for me this job is perfect. Sometimes getting out of show business for a short while and getting involved with another creative industry can be a smart idea. The idea that my feelings and taste are important can be very empowering."*

Contact

Contact any of the major modeling agencies and ask how they go about selecting their fit models. The actors' work program at Actors Equity sometimes gets calls for this type of work; check with them.

Shoe, Foot and Leg Model

Notes

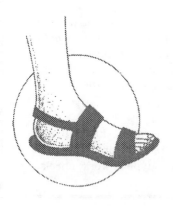

Shoe, Foot and Leg Model

Low Down
In this type of work, the models are hired because they have excellent legs and/or feet. For shoe shows, the model must be able to do runway work. For women, the length and shape of their legs determines how successful they'll be. Women must have a size 6 shoe, men an 8½ to do this work.

Scratch
$250-$300 per hour print, $300 a day live.

Be
- Know runway technique: how to walk with flair, and how to turn
- Have a pleasant personality
- Know how to pose feet and legs

Perks
- Free shoes
- Very good money
- No worry about overexposure, since faces are never shown

Bummers
- You must take extremely good care of your legs and feet. You can't get bruises; they must ALWAYS be in excellent condition
- Women leg models have short careers
- Runway work is tiring, especially on the feet

Horse's Mouth
David Roos, owner of Gilla Roos Models: *"This kind of work is a good addition to a model or actor's career. If you feel you have the qualifications for this work, by all means look into it."*

Contact
Gilla Roos Models, tel. (212) 727-7820. Any of the other major model agencies in New York or Los Angeles

Celebrity Impersonator

Notes

Horse's Mouth

An actress who does not want to be identified: *"I did Madonna for years, even before she got big, and for a while it was a fun gig. But once in a while there'd be the jerks, usually drunks, who didn't know real from make believe, and would start hitting on me, treating me like I was a tramp. It got crazy. I mean sometimes I'd be out on Long Island and, well it got very scary. So finally I gave her up. Now I do clown stuff at parties – no problems."*

Contact

New York Magazine lists many entertainment agencies that use celebrity impersonators. I suggest that you try calling several of them to find out who pays the most for your celebrity. The rates vary dramatically.

Celebrity Impersonator

Low Down

There are several types of celebrity impersonators:

Look-alike impersonators: only look like the celebrity. They are hired to walk around a party or event, mingling, taking photos, doing "shtick", and playing the role, but not performing. They are usually paid $150-$350 an hour.

Sing-alikes: actually sing and sound like the person they look like. They'll do a 20 minute show with a boom box or their own accompanist, and, if requested, walk around afterwards, mingling in character. They're paid anywhere from $350 an hour and up.

Lip-synch celebrity impersonators: not only look like the person but will also do a 20 minute show lip-synching some of that person's famous songs. These impersonators get $250 an hour and up.

One-of-a-kind (or rare) celebrity impersonators: are one of a kind or special. I was told there is only one major Jackie Gleason impersonator. He lives in L.A. and gets up to $7,500 (plus plane fare of course) a night.

Scratch

Varies widely, averaging from $150-$500 an hour.

Be

- Able to impersonate the celebrity VERY WELL—This means the look, the clothes, the walk, and the voice
- Friendly and outgoing in character
- If you do stage work, know all stage and microphone techniques
- If you do lip-synch or live singing, know all the hits of that celebrity

Perks

- The money is great
- Meet all kinds of people, go to all kinds of parties
- If you're successful as the celebrity, you get to feel the thrill of adoration
- If you're good, one party leads to many others and to television appearances

Bummers

- If your celebrity falls out of public favor, like Michael Jackson or Madonna, you'll work less
- People may think that's all you can do, which can be limiting

Theme Park Performer

Notes

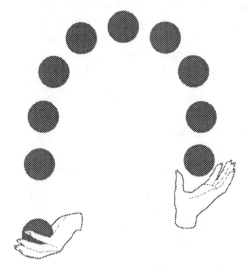

Contact

There are many theme parks all over the country, including:

- Walt Disney World
  Box 10,000
  Lake Buena Vista, FL 32830-1000

- Disneyland
  1313 Harbor Blvd
  Anaheim, CA 92803

- Disney-MGM Studios Theme Park
  Box 10,000
  Lake Buena Vista, FL 32830-1000
  (Talent Booking)

- Alan Albert Prods.
  561 Broadway, Suite 10C
  New York, NY 10012

Theme Park Performer

Low Down
If you're an entertainer (singer, dancer, musician, or actor) there is some kind of work for you at a theme park. Every year about 10 million people visit theme parks, so you're guaranteed to have an audience. The best known theme parks are open 365 days a year; most are only seasonal (spring through Labor Day). Some shows run only a half a minute long, others run for half an hour others all day long. The work is as varied as the types of theme parks themselves.

Scratch
Varies, averaging $250-$350 a week. Sometimes theme parks charge about $45 a week for housing.

Be
- Outgoing and friendly
- Able to deal with the public
- Comfortable working in a theme park environment
- Able to perform continuously in the same show

Perks
- Work in beautiful settings
- Use the park's facilities as much as you wish
- Meet people from all around the world
- In some theme parks there's steady work
- Some theme parks offer free classes in singing, dancing, and acting
- Some theme parks have a full medical plan
- Some theme parks offer paid vacations and sick days

Bummers
- You're unavailable for other acting work
- The noise and crowds can get to you after a while
- Theme parks are insistent on projecting a squeaky-clean persona
- After a while, the work can get monotonous
- The money is okay, but you'll never get rich doing this

Horse's Mouth
Renauld Morrison, an actor who has worked theme parks: *"When I was just starting out in the business, I did two summers of theme park work. Being among so many people was fun and exciting work. I was performing in a band five times a day playing banjo and singing. I found the work really thrilling. And you always had an appreciative audience, especially the kids."*

Cabaret Performer

Notes

Contact
There are many cabaret clubs in New York, including:

- Eighty Eight's
  228 West 10th Street
  New York, NY 10014

- Don't Tell Mama
  336 West 46th Street
  New York, NY 10036

- The Duplex
  61 Christopher Street
  New York, NY 10014

- Rainbow and Stars
  30 Rockefeller Plaza
  65th floor
  New York, NY 10020

Cabaret Performer

Low Down
The cabaret artist's world is usually a small stage in a nightclub. The room is smoke-filled and smells of liquor. In these small clubs, cabaret artists weave their magic: odd and unusual songs or popular ballads followed by a few minutes of patter and then more songs. The cabaret artist usually shares something personal with the audience.

Scratch
Varies widely: from a few dollars to hundreds for a show.

Be
- Comfortable close to, and intimate with, an audience
- Have a personal and cohesive feel to your act
- Choose the material and songs that will express what you are trying to say
- Have a different or unusual way to express yourself

Perks
- Intimate contact with an audience is very satisfying
- It can be a venue for bigger clubs, television, or theatre
- This type of work is very personal. Cabaret artists can express many of their feelings about life, and love
- As you develop a following, the money will improve

Bummers
- The room is crowded and smoke-filled
- The room may be empty
- Money is needed for photographs, mailings, and flyers
- Finding just the right song, the right patter, can be tough
- Developing a following takes years
- Getting critics to see you work is difficult. When they do, and don't like you, recovering is more difficult

Horse's Mouth
Jane Anne Williams, an actress who had a nightclub act: *"I never knew what the expression 'sweating bullets' meant until my first moment on a nightclub stage before an audience. The intimacy can be overwhelming. I mean they are right there, almost in your face, and you have to open your heart and sing. Once I got past that initial terrifying moment, I found it an incredibly warm and comfortable way to work, like being in your living room with close friends."*

Television Commercial Actor

Notes

Horse's Mouth

Yvette Minestre, an actress who does television commercials:
*"When you start to think about the money you can make in a
national McDonald's or orange juice spot, and think of how much
you're paid Off Broadway, it all seems surreal. Booking a national
spot is a real dream for me. Every time I read for a national, I feel
it's like buying a ticket to the lottery."*

Contact

The Ross Reports lists many of the talent agents, casting directors,
and production houses that use actors for television commercials.
The best way to contact them is with a photo and resumé (and a
note). Some of the schools that train for television commercials
include Bob Colliers, tel. (212) 929-4737, Weist-Barron, tel. (212)
840-7025, and The Three of Us Studios. You should take a class
before pursuing agents.

Television Commercial Actor

Low Down

To be successful in commercials, you must be an identifiable "type". Whether it's a mom or an executive, you must fit the American image. Aside from just being a "type", you must be able to sell a product. Whether it's the in-your-face, Crazy Eddie style commercials, or the soft approach used with feminine hygiene products, the more convincing you are, the more you'll work. At one time, serious actors scoffed at this type of work, but today many actors enjoy the money and high exposure. Again, "type" is key.

Scratch

Varies, depending on what type of work you do, and what market it plays. AFTRA wild spot rate is $443.25 for the session; AFTRA voice-over work rate is $311.50.

Be
- Able to find and emphasize the unique selling point within the copy
- Comfortable on-camera
- Work well under pressure
- Able to repeat the material over and over without getting frayed, take direction, and make adjustments, until the director and/or client are satisfied
- Personable, upbeat, and confident
- Totally believable and convincing as the type you're playing

Perks
- The money is very good
- Commercials are good exposure
- Some travel

Bummers
- The field is highly competitive
- The work can be grueling: especially if client and director aren't sure about what they want
- Sometimes you must make foolish copy seem brilliant

Theatrical Bookstore Employee

Notes

Horse's Mouth

Christopher Dailey, an actor who sold books for a short while:
"To me the best part of the job was when there weren't many people in the store and I could browse through a great play or find a new monologue. Just being surrounded by so much theater! I thought the job was pleasant and never felt too much pressure there."

Contact

The best way to find this work is to locate where the theatrical bookstores are and speak with the managers.

Theatrical Bookstore Employee

Low Down

Workers in theatrical bookstores assist customers by helping them find specific books or magazines. The job includes inventory work, arranging and shelving books, and other typical bookstore chores. Knowledge of plays, musical librettos, theatre, television, and film is necessary.

Scratch

Varies, starting at about $7 an hour.

Be
- Well acquainted with the theatre
- Able to remember titles of plays and books
- Able to suggest specific plays, books of monologues and other books depending on a customer's needs
- Friendly and outgoing

Perks
- Access to wonderful books on theatre, plays, etc.
- Meet all kinds of people in the business
- Flexible schedule
- Employers are generally actor-friendly

Bummers
- You're on your feet a lot
- Some people, no matter how hard you try, will never find what they're looking for
- Irate customers
- Dealing with several customers at one time patiently
- Each theater season brings new plays and music you must immediately become familiar with
- Some stores have late hours
- The money is not very good

Fight Director

Notes

Fight Director

Low Down
The fight director creates choreographed scenes of stage violence with guns or swords. He works with two or more people. He works on everything from contemporary and classical plays to movies. Part of the job is to collaborate with directors and designers. His work must be part of the play's concept. Occasionally, he is included in casting decisions.

Scratch
Varies widely, depending on where, what medium (theater, television, film), and what is required. Totally negotiable.

Be
- Patient, flexible and able to collaborate
- Have a good knowledge of historical weapons and fighting techniques
- Able to choreograph fighting in all periods and styles
- Know first aid
- Know tumbling, gymnastics, martial arts, and firearm safety
- In good physical shape

Perks
- It's very active, exciting work
- It's fun working with actors and seeing them learn to do the work
- Travel
- The work itself keeps you physically fit

Bummers
- This is freelance work: you never know when you'll be hired
- If you misrepresent yourself as an expert and someone gets hurt, you're liable
- It takes years to acquire these skills
- It takes years to develop a reputation in this field

Horse's Mouth
J. Allen Suddeth, an experienced fight director: *"Basically it's very exciting work. I find it very satisfying to work with so many people all over the country. Training, rehearsing the performers, and then seeing them do it so well in production is the best reward."*

Ed Easton, who has done this kind of work: *"The secret really is to make the actors look like they know hat they're doing; make them look like they've been doing it all their lives."*

Contact
The American Society of Fight Directors; tel. (800) 659-6579.

Performance Plus / Simulations Actor

Notes

Perks
- Travel all over the country
- Very interesting work
- No scripts to memorize
- The money is good
- Meet very interesting people in all kinds of professions

Bummers
- You never know when you'll be working
- You don't know what the job will be like (the space or the audience) until you get there
- You are categorized (Simulations) and called depending on your type
- Some of this work can be painful to portray: e.g. AIDS patients, or sexual harassment scenarios
- Often there is very technical information to learn

Horse's Mouth
Jay Raphael, a director with Simulations: *"This is a wonderful way for actors to earn money. The work is interesting and you deal with some very important issues."*

Bob Steed, owner of Performance Plus: *"We've found that the use of drama is a productive way to train people. Actors seem to find the work interesting and engaging."*

Contact
Performance Plus, Six Clark Lane, Suite 500, Rye, NY 10380.
Simulations, Box 399, 1470 Long Road, Martinsville, NJ 08836.

Performance Plus / Simulations Actor

Low Down

These two companies do much of the same type of work and employ many actors.

PERFORMANCE PLUS: Has been in business nearly six years. Topics addressed in their work include customer service, total quality management, supervisory training, sales training, sexual harassment and gender-related issues awareness. Clients include NYNEX, Con Edison, Pace University, Mutual of New York, Scholastic, and many others. Audience size ranges from 8 to 800. Programs last from 45 minutes to a full day. Formats include "after dinner programs", seminars/workshops, videos, and conferences/conventions. Much of the work is rehearsed improvisation work.

SIMULATIONS: Fifteen years in the business. Most of their casting is from files and referrals. They work with a slew of companies. 85% of their work is in the medical field (patient or doctor simulations). Their work is either live or on video. They work mostly with union actors under union contracts (AEA, AFTRA, SAG). Their work is rehearsed improvisation. One aspect of what they do is the use of videos to demonstrate to doctors the correct and incorrect procedures. The format here is similar to industrial films. They look for actors who can be behavioral specialists for their type of work.

Scratch

Varies widely, averaging $350 a day and up.

Be

- Trained in improv
- A sales background is helpful for *Performance Plus*
- Quick on your feet
- Friendly and outgoing
- Able to do ensemble work
- Comfortable on camera
- Take direction well and be able to adjust your work at any moment
- Feel comfortable interacting, in character, with the audience after the show

Perfume Squirter at Department Stores

Notes

Contact

There are several ways to get this work: Contact the individual cosmetics company. Go to the cosmetic counter at a department store and inquire. Check with personnel at the department store to see if they hire perfume squirters. Try On Call Promotional Personnel, 30 East 42nd Street, Room 200, New York, NY 10017.

Perfume Squirter at Department Stores

Low Down

In this job women (or men) stand in the aisles of department stores and, with permission, spray passersby. The point of this work is to allow customers to sample perfume or cologne, and then sell it to them.

Scratch

Varies, generally $10-$20 an hour.

Be
- Have good sales skills
- Friendly, outgoing
- Attractive and well-groomed
- Very verbal, very vocal

Perks
- You are an independent contractor, so you set your own schedule
- This is a nice way to meet people
- You have the opportunity to work for different companies: if you don't like the one you're working for, try another

Bummers
- You're on your feet a lot
- You have to deal with irate customers
- You're not guaranteed work all the time
- Spraying that much perfume all the time can turn you off to the scent, make it difficult to sell
- You're hired back dependent on your sales production, so you're always under the gun

Horse's Mouth

Naomi Lindler, an actress who does this work: *"I enjoy this work. I've met some very lovely people and find that the time just flies by. It's not really difficult, and I find that if you're really nice to women, and men, they'll stop and take the time to investigate your fragrance and, hopefully, buy."*

Industrial and Commercial Extra

Notes

Contact

For commercial extra work, get the Ross Reports: it tells which ad agencies and commercial casting directors accept photos for extra work. Also check out the production houses to see who keeps an extras file. Industrial films are a little trickier. There are some casting directors who book industrial extras: find out who they are, and if they accept photos, SEND them!

Industrial and Commercial Extra

Low Down
Both commercial and industrial films use extra players. Their purpose
is to give a scene a more realistic feel. Extras should be seen and not
heard (especially when there's a boom mike around). Extras cross in
front of and behind the principles. It may be a scene in a restaurant
or at the office; there may be only two extras or twenty. Extra players
dress up a set so it doesn't look empty and "unlived in." Extras are
generally typed by category: e.g. upscale, or blue collar.

Scratch
$240 for limited run commercials (13 weeks); $366 for unlimited
run commercials; $99 for industrials.

Be
- Experienced on-camera
- Have a good, well varied wardrobe
- Know how to mime a conversation
- As in all on-camera work, movements should not be too big
- Other commercial or industrial extra work is helpful

Perks
- In commercials, the money is the best of all extra work
- Generally, the food on commercials is better than at other extra work
- Commercial extras sometimes have a shot at being upgraded to a principle
  role. On a national spot, that's big bucks!

Bummers
- Being seen as an extra is not always the best thing for an ambitious actor.
  Some people look down on this kind of work
- If you do too much commercial extra work and become recognizable, it may
  preclude you from getting principle work later on

Horse's Mouth
Lenore Rosen, an actress who has done both commercial and
industrial extra work: *"Although I've done both, you can give me
commercial extra work any day. You're usually treated very well
and the food's always great. I find however, that I get much more
industrial extra work. I've hooked up with a couple of industrial film
directors who'll call me if they're shooting in town. As for
commercial extras, I seem to get called by the same production
houses every few months for a job."*

Camera Operator

Notes

Contact

Check with individual video or production houses to see if they're looking for apprentices. Cable television is the new venue for finding work in this field. Many beginning camera operators are finding training and work in independent video productions.

Camera Operator

Low Down
This job entails the physical operation of a camera for television or film. The two most commonly used cameras are the "hard" camera, which weighs several hundred pounds and rests on a movable platform or pedestal, and the "minicam", which rests on the shoulders, usually weighs about 40 pounds, and is used mostly on remotes. This kind of work is both technical and creative.

Scratch
Varies, depending on where and whether you're doing video or film. Generally, $35 an hour on union films, $350 a day for network television.

Be
- Able to pay special attention to detail
- Able to work well under pressure
- Have an eye for framing the picture
- Film making is a collaborative process: be able to work well with all the other technicians and artists
- Camera operators quite often learn on the job

Perks
- You can make very good money as you advance
- Frequent travel
- A chance to meet the movers and shakers in motion pictures: actors, directors, producers

Bummers
- The field is very competitive
- Starting salaries can be very low
- The work is irregular.
- Work under a lot of pressure
- These jobs mostly go to men
- The work can be physically demanding, so you need to be in good shape

Horse's Mouth
Harold Kliener, a former motion picture camera operator:
"Although I enjoyed the hustle-bustle of film making, the days can be very long and the work grueling. Camera operators should understand lenses, lighting, and how balance works in a frame."

Music Therapist

Notes

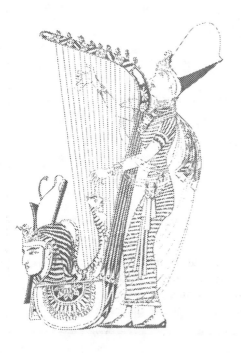

Music Therapist

Low Down
Music therapists help people who are emotionally blocked express themselves through music. They primarily work in hospitals and nursing homes or privately in people's homes. They help people "come out of themselves" with music. The belief here is that, with music as a catalyst, the patient will be able to recall emotions and memories that have been severely blocked. The music therapist works in collaboration with psychiatrists, psychologists, and physical therapists (when dealing with the handicapped.) The music therapist can work with groups or on a one-to-one basis.

Scratch
Varies, averaging $15,000-$40,000 full-time, between $10 and $20 an hour part-time.

Be
- Have a bachelor's degree in music
- Have at least two years training as an intern in this field
- Very patient with clients' progress
- Have an excellent knowledge of music
- Have a genuine concern for clients

Perks
- Part-time workers make their own schedules
- It's a way to help people
- Seeing a client have an emotional break-through is satisfying
- This is a very creative form of therapy

Bummers
- The work can be very frustrating
- It can be difficult to find work in this field
- To make better money in this field, more training and experience are necessary. This can be very time consuming

Horse's Mouth
Nancy Hoffman, an actress who has been a music therapist:
"It was very gratifying to see a client finally have a break-through. When you work so closely with someone and see them finally break down that door... it's really a wonderful moment."

Contact
National Association of Music Therapists. American Association of Music Therapists.

Reader for the Elderly

Notes

Reader for the Elderly

Low Down
In this work, actors go to the home or hospital of the client and read from books, articles, and letters, aloud. The reader is generally employed because the clients are blind or partially blind or too ill to read to themselves. The reader must find out if the client wishes to have the work read softly or with "dramatic flair".

Scratch
Varies widely, averaging $7-$10 an hour for a two hour minimum.

Be
- Sensitive to the demands of the elderly
- Enjoy reading, sometimes for long stretches
- Comfortable reading all styles of writing from novels to poetry

Perks
- This can be very relaxing work
- This can be emotionally rewarding work
- Your schedule is flexible
- You receive constant referrals, can work for many people

Bummers
- Sometimes the elderly can be difficult
- If the client becomes severely ill or dies, it can be emotionally difficult for the reader
- Clients may cancel a session at the last minute

Horse's Mouth
Rolanda San Croix, an actress who's done this work: *"I found this to be one of the most wonderful jobs I've ever had. Some of my people were so giving and kind, I'll never forget them. Some were so pure and sweet it was like working with tiny children."*

Contact
The best way to get this work is through word-of-mouth, bulletin boards, and local newspapers. Organizations such as Hadassah only use volunteers for this work.

Theater Usher

Notes

Theater Usher

Low Down
The theater usher's job is to help members of an audience find their seats before and during a show. In some theaters, there is one who is assigned to look at the audience member's tickets and send them to the correct section. It's also the usher's duty to make sure each person receives a program. If there are any problems regarding an audience member's seat, the usher must handle it quickly, quietly, and in a polite manner. After the show, the usher makes sure the audience members know where the closest exits are.

Scratch
Varies, averaging about $10 an hour.

Be
- Familiar with the theater. Aside from the seating area, you must know where the bathrooms, phones, bar, and exits are.
- Polite and courteous
- Able to quickly and quietly get late arrivals to their seats

Perks
- The job is not too difficult
- See the show
- Sometimes, but rarely, there are tips
- You may meet celebrities, stars
- The hours are short

Bummers
- People changing their seats create annoying problems
- Dealing with irate and/or loud audience members
- On your feet and going up and down stairs a lot
- Sometimes it's difficult to get this work

Horse's Mouth
Sylvia Kennedy, who has been doing this work for over 20 years: *"I'll tell you, I've met some of the most wonderful people doing this work. But it's really changed over the years. At one time everyone dressed up, was respectful, and there were a lot more tips. Today, well, it's still nice work, and when you're in a theater with a hit show you can work for a long time. Think of the ushers over at Cats!"*

Contact
International Alliance of Theatrical Stage Employees (IATSE), theater ushers local.

Broadcast Time Salesperson

Notes

Contact
The best way to find this work is by contacting the station
directors. In this field, they are always hiring, so you have a good
chance to find a job. Check out Advertising Age and Cable World.
Write to the Radio Advertising Bureau, 304 Park Avenue South,
New York, NY 10010.

Broadcast Time Salesperson

Low Down
The broadcast time salesperson sells television or radio commercials. It is the money from this work that keeps the television or radio station on the air. The time salesperson (also called account executive or sales representative) must convince clients of the advertising value of their radio or television network. Usually, people starting out in this field begin at the local level, at a small radio station or cable television network. It's not only getting the clients that's important, it's keeping them.

Scratch
Varies widely, depending on the medium, the network, and the area.

Be
- Self-motivated and ambitious
- Have excellent people skills
- Able to listen to a client's needs and persuade them that what your station has to offer is the solution
- Know computers: most stations use them for this type of work
- Know all about commercials
- Friendly and outgoing

Perks
- The money is good if you're successful
- As you move up, you're given liberal expense accounts for entertaining your clients

Bummers
- You may experience a lot of rejection in this field
- It may take a while before you start making good money
- You're under constant pressure to produce
- Income is unsteady

Horse's Mouth
Joe Lantry, an actor who has done this work: *"If you start connecting with clients you can really rake the money in. The problem I had was all the rejection. It's not like you don't get enough of it (rejection) in show business, but then in your part-time job too? I did it for about two years, made some good money."*

Trade Show Actor

Notes

Trade Show Actor

Low Down

Trade shows hire actors, singers, dancers, spokespersons, etc. There is always sufficient work in this field. Performers are generally hired for 8-10 hour shifts with a one hour break or two or three half-hour breaks. This work includes on-going presentations at the trade show as long as the show is in town. Shows include automobile shows, gift shows, toy shows, and others.

Scratch

Varies widely, depending on skills, show, and client.

Be
- Adept in whatever field you're hired in
- Have stamina: it is a long day with continuous presentations
- Dependable and reliable
- Able to interact with business people
- Well groomed and attractive
- Articulate and confident
- Some jobs require a tuxedo or evening wear

Perks
- You can usually find work in this field, especially in New York
- If you're experienced and well known, the money can be good
- This is a great way to meet people
- Some agencies pay daily

Bummers
- The work can be grueling: you're on your feet for up to ten hours doing on-going shows
- Sometimes there's a lot of material to learn
- On occasion the material is embarrassing. This ain't art, it's business

Horse's Mouth

A representative from On Call Promotional Personnel, an agency that has been hiring trade show talent for over 25 years: *"If you're talented and want to make some extra money in this field, there certainly is sufficient work. Many of our people say they find the work fun and interesting."*

Contact

On Call Promotional Personnel, 30 East 42nd Street, Room 200, New York, NY 10017. Or call other promotional employment agencies.

Script Reader

Notes

Script Reader

Low Down
The script reader's job is to read through scripts for different organizations. For movies and television, you may also be expected to read the novel a script is based on. Sometimes you're doing an initial reading in a contest to see if the script should be passed on to final judges; other times a theater company hires you to determine if the script should be eligible for their next season. Each organization has it's own format for critiquing. Usually the reader must write a synopsis, a critique, and a recommendation.

Scratch
Varies: about $5-$15 per script for theater, $20-$50 for television or movies.

Be
- Be able to critique a script objectively
- Be a fast but thorough reader
- Have a strong liberal arts background

Perks
- You get to know a lot of writers
- You can develop good contacts with theaters, and producing groups
- If you have come across a good script and it gets produced, you're already familiar with the material. Now all you need is an audition
- You work when you want to work

Bummers
- You're sometimes given up to ten scripts at a time and have to shlep them all over town
- You have to read a lot of bad plays
- This type of work can get monotonous
- This work can be very time consuming for very little money

Horse's Mouth
Seth Gordon, director and associate producer at Primary Stages: *"What's wonderful about this work is that sometimes you discover an exciting new playwright and can help to bring his work recognition."*

Hair Model

Notes

Hair Model

Low Down

Hair models are hired to have their hair cut and/or bleached, dyed, or styled, for hair trade shows or hair magazines. There is far more work for women here, but some for men also.

Scratch

About $300 per day, plus a free haircut and styling from the client at a later date.

Be
- Have beautiful, easy to manage hair
- For print work, have print modeling experience
- Willing to cut your hair as short as need be for the job

Perks
- You get a free haircut and styling. Most hair salons will give you another free haircut and styling at a later date if you wish
- It's a way to start an on-going relationship with a hair salon or hair company which may bring you future work
- If you want to change your look, you can be paid to develop a new look

Bummers
- If you do print modeling regularly, the haircut may be so severe you'll be put out of commission for many months
- You may not like how you look, but you're stuck with it
- This work is limited. Once your long hair is cut short, you may not get another job from the client until it grows back

Horse's Mouth

Donna Wolfson, a commercial print model who does this work:
"I'm very specific about who and what I'll allow done with my hair. I have certain hair clients that I've worked with off and on for years. They're usually only in town for the hair show. If I'm available and they call I usually book the day with them. With other hair clients I have to have a very specific agreement as to what I will or will not allow to be done to my hair."

Contact

Most major model agencies "dabble" in this type of work. Call to find out what requirements they have.

Body Parts Model

Notes

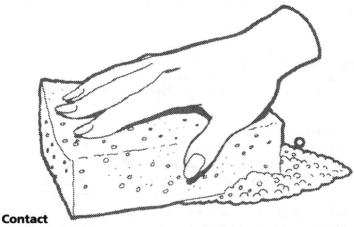

Contact
Most major commercial print agencies handle body parts calls. For
physique body parts: if you have an excellent, well-defined body
and are interested in this type of work, contact Better Bodies
Models Management, Inc., 22 West 19th Street, New York NY. Tel.
(212) 620-3197.

Body Parts Model

Low Down
This print modeling work includes any and all parts of the human anatomy. Models receive print assignments for everything from their ears and ear lobes to knees to well developed pecs or forearms. Interestingly enough, there is a substantial amount of this work. Men and women with well-defined bodies are making excellent money for all their hard work, especially in health, weight lifting, and nutrition magazines. Odd calls come in to agencies all the time for very specific body parts for all kinds of products.

Scratch
Varies, starting about $250 an hour.

Be
- Comfortable in front of a camera no matter what body part you are modeling
- Have modeling skills
- Keep the body part unbruised and unblemished
- Keep in excellent condition

Perks
- Since it's a specific body part that's being photographed (usually not including the face), there is no concern about overexposure
- Since the face isn't shown, you won't have any product conflicts
- With physique body parts you work more often than with other body parts. The market is constantly improving
- Personal satisfaction and gain for all the work you've put in at the health club

Bummers
- The work is irregular
- You can't build a career on this type of work, although physique body parts is a growing field
- If you're doing physique body parts, you must be absolutely religious about diet and work outs. Those pecs or forearms must always be "camera-ready"

Horse's Mouth
Kurt Leopold, a weight trainer, model, and actor: *"I'm just getting into this body parts work, and already my forearms and biceps have been photographed several times for national magazines. After so many years of hard training, it feels great. The money is super and the work's easy"*